Dr. Rebecca Hardcastle takes the next fascinating step towards addressing the intelligences behind unexplained phenomena and beyond. While incorporating her own intimate journey of discovery, she assists and nurtures the reader to experience theirs. "It is the light and so much more".

—Lynne D. Kitei, MD, Author and Executive Producer
The Phoenix Lights…We Are Not Alone

Exoconsciousness invites us to share our stories and to find our true inner peace, so that as a human species we can wisely and lovingly reconnect with our Cosmic Families who have been patiently waiting our awakening. Dr. Hardcastle has written the definitive book for peace on Earth and peace in Space.

—Terri Mansfield, Executive Director and Co-founder
Arizona Department of Peace Campaign

For the longest time, Rebecca Hardcastle has been doing pioneer work in consciousness research, integrating spirituality and quantum physics. She speaks of humanity in the new millennia and how the human mind will awaken to be "alive as an energetic being, awakened through spiritual arts." It is a must -read for all those wishing to transcend our human limitations and enter the Cosmic Age.

—Paola Harris, Author and UFO Researcher
Exopolitics: How does One Speak to a Ball of Light?
Connecting the Dots: Making Sense of the UFO Phenomena

Exopolitics, New Energy, and Exo-Consciousness are the three pillars of the Universal era humanity is entering. Rebecca Hardcastle's book, *ExoConciousness*, provides a vocabulary for consciousness in this new era.

—Alfred Lambremont Webre, JD, MEd, Author, *Exopolitics: Politics, Government and Law in the Universe*; International Director
Institute for Cooperation in Space (ICIS), www.exopolitics. com.

Rebecca Hardcastle's work, *Exoconsciousness: Your 21st Century Mind* is indeed a wondrous voyage of the mind, spirit and body. Her imagery is breath-taking. Reaching into the depths of her own soul, Rebecca caresses the deepest intimacy of the reader's mind as she reaches to touch the stars.

—Victor Viggiani, MEd, Director of Media Relations Exopolitics Toronto.

Dr. Hardcastle has effectively introduced a concept and a vocabulary that moves us forward into a future that transition into the 21st Century requires.

—Dr. Ruth Hover, Psychotherapist/Abduction Research

Dr. Hardcastle has forged from her own illuminating and precious resource of consciousness, an essential meet-and-greet holistic "primer" for our official entry into the multitude of intergalactic and inter-dimensional cultures. Don't leave Earth without it.

—Jeff Peckman, Denver Extraterrestrial Affairs Commission Ballot Initiative

Rebecca Hardcastle's work is a perfect guide to human race, which looks for the spiritual essence in a physical dimension on our cosmic journey.

—Farah Yurdozu, UFO Investigator and Writer

A compelling, beautifully written, high-energy journey by an author thoroughly familiar with the wide range of subject materials informing what she calls "exoconsciousness." Indeed, the fundamental difference between what the adepts of the 60s called *cosmic consciousness* and Hardcastle's *exoconsciousness* is that the latter term incorporates neuro-scientific and technological utility whereas cosmic consciousness remains hopelessly vague and tends towards world negation. A fundamental issue raised by Hardcastle's rich tableau of personal experiences, however, as well as her account of the experiences of others, has to do with the hermeneutics of testimony. In short, how does one critically evaluate matters of *attestation?* How does one determine the veracity of the testimony of witnesses or the witnesses of witnesses? Until this question is answered suitably, the evidentiary testimony of paranormal experiences remains indeterminate apart from falling into yet another form of fideism. Hardcastle clearly wants to avoid this trap, her point of view is anything but world-negating, and her book is a positive step in determining what kind of consciousness is required for constructive human development into the 21st century and beyond.

—Alan M. Olson, Professor, Philosophy of Religion, Boston University

Rebecca not only shares her unique personal experience of awakening in *Exoconsciousness*, she provides us with a detailed roadmap that allows each of us to further explore the reality of conceptual consciousness. Her journey is heightened by ancient legacies and visionary insight that allows the reader to tie together the fragmented, multi-dimensional world in which we exist.

—Brit Elders, Author, Investigator, CEO of ShirleyMacLaine.com

This is an autobiography of a woman who came from light and health to darkness and pain. It is her journey to a barely imaginable existence within light and health of an entirely different kind. It is also a Kerouacian tour de force of what we are, how we think and the things around us we don't notice.

—Jay Kappmeier, Colonel (Ret), United States Air Force.

"Exo" will be the prefix of this century. Exobiology, exopolitics, exoscience, exoarcheology, exoconsciousness - these terms will assert their presence in a world of post-formal disclosure of a non-human intelligence, most likely extraterrestrial in origin, engaging the human race. Every person who has intersected with this non-human intelligence has been changed. Rebecca Hardcastle is one such person. She advances the concept of exoconsciousness from deep personal experience and a strong feminine perspective.

—Stephen Bassett, Paradigm Research Group

Whether you are well versed in the subject matter or brand new, *Exoconsciousness*, is a must read. It is crucial at this time in our planet's history that stories like Dr. Hardcastle's be heard.

—Katie Cook, Television Host

Dr. Hardcastle presents a masterful survey of contemporary understandings about the conscious mind, which she then applies to such diverse and important areas as mental travel through time, processing encounters with Visitors from the stars, and accomplishing healing by focused mental concentration. A brilliant tour-de-force!"
> —Richard Boylan, PhD, LLC, Councilor, President,
> Star Kids Project, Ltd

Few writers have made the leap that consciousness is a phenomenon from and of space beyond earth. Exoconsciousness transcends the homocentric confinement, which limits the usual discussion of conscious phenomena. Dr. Hardcastle takes us on a ride to a far place of human evolution, and from that vantage point shows us where —and who— we really are.
> —Larry Lowe, Network Developer
> Homo-luminous.net, Exoeconomics.net

Exoconsciousness

Your 21st Century Mind

Rebecca Hardcastle, PhD

AuthorHouse™
1663 Liberty Drive, Suite 200
Bloomington, IN 47403
www.authorhouse.com
Phone: 1-800-839-8640

First published by AuthorHouse 12/19/2008

ISBN: 978-1-4389-2719-0 (sc)

Library of Congress Control Number: 2008911371

Printed in the United States of America
Bloomington, Indiana

This book is printed on acid-free paper.

For my legacy of Star children
Christopher, Kerry, Elizabeth, Catherine, David,
Andrew, Brent, Jeremy,
Rebecca, Abigail, Alexandra, Adam, Sarah, Lane,
Layla and Lucia

Gratitude for the Stars who form my Constellation
Michele, Ruth, Ed, Don, Mary Kay, Lynne, Terri, Larry, Perry,
Sarah, Marc, David and Beth

Editor, Robin di Perna
Cover Art, Larry Lowe

TABLE OF CONTENTS

Are you going to tell them you talk to dead people?
Yes.

Are you going to tell them you talk to extraterrestrials?
Yes.

Are you going to tell them you talk to beings without bodies?
Yes.

Can I listen?

Introduction

I walk among worlds—a world of everyday life, a world of loved ones who have passed over, a world of beings that dwell dimensionally next to earth, and a world of inter-dimensional extraterrestrials. As I walk between worlds I physically sense presences, recognize personalities, hear communications, smell aromas, and see energies.

In this book I share my travels in these worlds—preparation, experiences, and relationships that became my path. I explore scientific theories of consciousness and historic, scientific evidence that validate and explain my experiences. This journey of knowledge broadened my understanding of who I am as an early 21st Century human on planet Earth, living in a universe teaming with accessible, intelligent life.

In another era, sharing my communication between worlds might not have been as acceptable. History is fraught with stories of persecution, prejudice, and strange silence regarding inter-dimensional communication. Today, it is permissible, even scientifically acceptable.

Like a submerged vessel, a body of knowledge is rising within human consciousness. Memory is reconnecting lost fragments. As our bodies integrate more recovered fragments of knowledge we can use them to evolve, heal, create, and reconnect to a source that vibrates with the comfort, safety, protection, and familiarity of home.

As humans reconnect to inter-dimensional sources, science facilitates the convergence. **Quantum physics** explores multi-dimensional theories of reality on sub-atomic levels. Energy exchanges witnessed;

unusual scientific laws operative. For example, the quantum theory of **entanglement** predicts that sub-atomic particles at a distance, once related, continue to reference each other. As such, scientists predict particle relationships within a degree of mathematical certainty. Entanglement is a far cry from Newtonian mechanistic science that separated and analyzed, without a thought to the interconnected nature of our universe.

Exploring sub-atomic reality calls into question not only sacrosanct scientific theories; it modifies our view of reality. Today, scientists extrapolate multi-dimensional reality using a myriad of mathematical equations, spectacular experiments with supercolliders, and formulas ratified by next generation computers. As quantum theories develop, human experience, validated in the fields of parapsychology and paranormal, garners respect and attention.

Quantum physics determined that we live in a multi-dimensional reality through scientific experiments and accompanying mathematical theories. The next step for scientists is to acknowledge inter-dimensional, intelligent beings that dwell in these worlds that I walk. What science explores with precise, belabored measurements, human consciousness senses with ease. Our earth home, our human bodies, our minds, and our spirits are in a period of rapid evolvement. In the early 21st Century, human consciousness and its inherent power, abilities, skills, and connections may determine the future of our planet and our people. *Consciousness is our most precious human resource.*

Conceptualizing consciousness is a distinctive endeavor. Unlike other scientific research, consciousness requires more than objective experimentation, rigorous research, or infallible doctrine. Consciousness research requires subjectivity balanced with objectivity. It demands personal involvement, no matter how bizarre, no matter how chaotic, no matter how challenging. Consciousness research demands personal, intimate experience.

Mining the resource of human consciousness requires courage to share. Some of my story may seem "other worldly" or bizarre. It is. The study of consciousness is chaotic, bizarre, beautiful, structured, and more. Take what you wish of the stories. Leave the rest. Balance the stories with scientific research and ancient wisdom. Experiment with the exercises; see if they work for you. All are given in a spirit of love and commitment to the source that dwells within each human—the source that lights our way.

It is the purpose of this book to glimpse the workings of human consciousness through personal experience, scientific research, and ancient knowledge in order to gain a clearer understanding of who we are as humans and how best we can manage and use our consciousness.

Let's get started with a brief orientation that includes "rules for the road." This manual will prepare you for the journey. Exoconsciousness is primarily personal. As such, attention to your personal vehicle, prior to journey, is essential.

Rules for the Road

My story began with my life out of balance. I was lopsided. I needed to learn how to rebalance and align the energies of my mind, body, and spirit. As my period of adjustment unfolded, I soon learned that humans possess a delicate energy system that requires ongoing maintenance and technical knowledge.

During my career in job placement at a technical school I worked with a team of automotive instructors. Placing young technicians, I learned to value the intricacies of their high-tech craft. They keep us moving. Humans are a vehicle, and like a car, require servicing, rebalancing, and alignment to move in a straight path. Yet, detours and stops are savored. Our compass is consulted. Observing the rules of the road assures sure, steady directional movement.

Rule 1: Balance

Healthy human bodies operate most effectively in a state of perfect balance. Yin and yang, dark and light, male and female strive for perfect balance. This balance permits both sides of your duality to open and thrive. Set aside judgment and criticism. Accept and love both sides of your balance. Like separating an egg yolk from the white, we often pull apart our natural balance, believing one aspect of our balance will harm us. We question our psychic ability to read energies, intuit answers, or communicate with other dimensions. We believe these abilities will harm our ability to live a productive, present, successful life.

One side of your human potential enriches the other. Harm lies in separation, not balance. When select human behaviors are separated, moralized, and demonized your internal balance further tilts out of alignment. Rules of balance require all aspects of your human nature to be unified, nurtured, healed, and affirmed.

Rule 2: Alignment

Alignment is intentional. As beings gifted with freedom of will and movement, each moment of your life is pregnant with choice. Yes or no. Here or there. This or that. We define the flow of our life by the choices of where, when, how, and with whom we align. Later in the book, I share exercises that strengthen alignment. Much anxiety and stress of everyday life can be simply and effortlessly allayed through intentional alignment. Choose your direction and your intention unfolds.

Rule 3: Filter

Change your filter frequently. Clean and clear energy movement is essential. Our internal filter protects us from harmful elements and sour fumes that fill our environment. Others' toxicity need not be absorbed. Use your healthy filter to block the spewing fumes of another's anger, anxiety, and fear. Protect your balance and alignment using your healthy, powerful filter system that is unafraid to block unwanted energies. We are created with an internal protection system that is essential for our evolution and growth in a peaceful environment we have created.

Rule 4: Fuel

Diet and exercise fuel the human engine of body, mind, and spirit. Careful attention to what goes into your body results in higher octaves of vibration and higher states of energy combustion. Because many food fuels are available and many experts ready to design your fuel mixture, the bottom line is that you, often through trial and error, design your perfect diet and exercise routine. Your body will respond when the mixture is perfect for you. Trust yourself.

Rule 5: Servicing

Just as servicing an engine removes sludge; your human engine requires frequent, routine cleansing to remove impurities. Cleansing is an ongoing essential process. Your mind accelerates when cleansed of thoughts no longer needed or beliefs no longer valid. Your body flourishes when cleansed of toxins that block and poison your system. Your spirits soar, relieved of accumulated energies that hold you back and form an invisible barrier preventing movement. Cleansing and servicing teach us to dwell peacefully in the void, an empty vessel. We become a bowl ready to receive the blessings of our world. Just as with diet, many experts are ready to design your cleanse. Your body recognizes the perfect mixture. Trust yourself.

Rule 6: Combustion

When your fuel mixture is perfect and your engine serviced, then a natural spark of energy flows continuously through your body. It is a rare gift, literally a divine spark. It sparks whether we are aware of it or not. Once we recognize its force we naturally want to nurture and tune it on a daily basis. Some link our spark to **Kundalini**, the yoga practice that links energy and consciousness to universal source through breathing and movement. This Kundalini energy rests in the fertile region of your sexual organs. Awakened, it pours its power through you. Feeling it awaken and flow through your being is one of the power experiences of being human. You are alive. You are connected. You are awake and aware of a vast energy system that surrounds you. As humans, we participate in this energy system every moment. But unlike mechanical vehicles, our limitless spark generates now and forever. We are an eternal energy flow that moves inter-dimensionally as well as through daily earth life.

Rule 7: Reading the Manual

Throughout this book I write in a language of symbols and images. Inter-dimensional and extra-dimensional knowledge is poetic and mathematical. If the language confuses you, simply close your eyes, relax, and allow your whole being to understand. As you relax, your subconscious mind easily translates meaning to your conscious mind. Since many exoconscious terms are unfamiliar, I italicized select words and included them in the glossary. Be patient with yourself. Absorb the information slowly and easily. There is no need to rush or feel anxious. Dimensional awareness is as human as breathing and laughter.

Exoconsciousness Orientation

The concept of exoconsciousness is the protagonist of this book. One morning, the word exoconsciousness manifested in my mind. It felt perfect. One word simplified my journey of conceptualizing consciousness. It harmonized and unified a rather chaotic, bizarre jumble of experiences. Creating the concept of exoconsciousness stirred and shifted my reality into a new pattern.

Exoconsciousness describes the extraterrestrial legacy, dimensions, and abilities of human consciousness. It characterizes the innate ability of our human consciousness to communicate, travel, and use extraterrestrial abilities such as intuition, telepathy, astral travel, *remote viewing*, manifestation, and ***teleportation***. We experience our extraterrestrial legacy of exoconsciousness as we communicate and travel among dimensions that are inter-connected and one with humans. Specifically, the field of exoconsciousness incorporates the study of extraterrestrial ***contactees*** and ***experiencers*** as it relates to consciousness. It incorporates biological research into the possible extraterrestrial imprints in human DNA. It also incorporates religious, mythological, and historical research of ancient and ongoing extraterrestrial contact; as well as contemporary consciousness, mind, and brain research.

Exoconsciousness complements UFO and extraterrestrial fields of research such as ***ufology*** and ***exopolitics***. Ufology, an established research field, is the study of extraterrestrial phenomenon, such as craft sightings, landings, alien visitation, and contact experience. Ufologists are primarily concerned with establishing definitive empirical evidence of UFOs and extraterrestrial visitation. Through the dedication of ufologists, massive databases of sightings, landings, and contact are readily accessible. Ufologists comb archives, request documents through the Freedom of Information Act, and travel (often at their own expense) to interview witnesses and visit research sites. They face an often thankless, daunting task.

Empirical science is reductionist. Most mainline scientists and academicians hold the simple answer—we have been and continue to be visited by extraterrestrials—in abeyance. For them, empirical extraterrestrial proof remains elusive. A silent divide separates ufologists from the mainstream. And yet, as empirical evidence mounts—a tipping point is in sight.

Unlike ufology, which emerged after WWII during heightened mass sightings, exopolitics is relatively recent. Exopolitics examines the most reliable information regarding UFOs and extraterrestrials through political and historical frameworks, concentrating on the importance of disclosure as a political reality. Exopolitics is primarily concerned with the implications—historical, political, and social—of the best available evidence of extraterrestrial visitation. As disclosure unfolds, exopolitics investigates the evidence, examines the implications, and proposes diplomatic protocols for contact. It also focuses on the mounting evidence of a quasi-governmental cover-up and manipulation of extraterrestrial information. Michael Salla, founder of the Exopolitics Institute, and Alfred Webre, director of the Institute for Cooperation in Space are pioneers of exopolitics.

Exoconsciousness, while closely linked to ufology and exopolitics, examines the implications for human consciousness in extraterrestrial contact and visitation. It is primarily concerned with legitimizing the participants or witnesses of extraterrestrial contact. It examines the philosophical, psychological, religious, and biological implications of the contact experiences, its ensuing information, and impact on human consciousness. Furthermore, it focuses on the implications of mind control, whether through established mainline institutions, scientific research, or media management.

Exoconsciousness proposes theories of extraterrestrial-based human consciousness accompanied by transformations in the human belief system. It is poised to provide information that will assist humans in the necessary endeavor of dismantling and transforming ineffective, outmoded belief systems. In addition, it will assist with the creation of new belief systems, compatible with the human species' emergence as a space faring, extraterrestrial race.

A next generation storyteller, both intuitive and detail oriented, I want to share the panorama, the big picture, along with the fascinating detail. I want you to become familiar with what I mean by exoconsciousness as you move through my story and the stories of others. I want you to understand my academic as well as my subjective orientation.

In 2005 I taught Extraterrestrial Reality, one of the first college-sponsored ufology courses in the nation, at Scottsdale Community College in Arizona through the Community Education Department. The college and local media embraced the course, publicizing it on television, radio, and in the print media. The class had a high caliber of students, many with contact experience and a broad intellectual knowledge of the science, history, and metaphysics surrounding UFOs and extraterrestrial visitation.

The Scottsdale Community College Extraterrestrial Reality course was designed to expand on the idea of what it means to be human in the 21st Century, as we relate to forms of intelligent, responsive life originating or occurring beyond or within Earth dimensions. Ufology was presented as an academic body of knowledge. Conceptual knowledge was combined with hands-on, competency-based learning. Participants were encouraged to share and expand on their experiences in a safe, non-judgmental environment. All styles of learning and subjective experiences were respected.

Why is an academic UFO, extraterrestrial curriculum necessary? Because, it provides a body of knowledge that may be used to understand current news and cultural events. In some news markets, such as Phoenix, the media embraces UFO reports. Nightly newscasts of sightings and contact experience boost audience ratings. A background in ufology, exopolitics, and exoconsciousness are essential in separating wheat from chaff, illusory from possible, and staged from actual. As scientific theories from fields like quantum physics and zero point energy emerge from the subatomic realm into the mainstream, a UFO, extraterrestrial-based curriculum easily accommodates our new reality. As extraterrestrial reality becomes culturally pervasive, individuals have a touchstone, an objective body of respected research, to use in examining their subjective experiences.

Subjective experience is recognized as an integral part of ufology, exopolitics, and exoconsciousness. As participants create their extraterrestrial reality, it is necessary to lean on subjective experience to integrate objective information.

My reality shifted while attending the 2005 X-Conference in Washington, D.C. Jaime Maussan, fondly known as "Mexico's Mike Wallace" of *60 Minutes*, presented a compilation of UFO videos that had been sent by his viewing audience. During one of his videos, I watched a morphing mother ship, suspended in space, simultaneously digest and launch hundreds of craft. I intuitively sensed that these craft were not the technological nuts and bolts of our aerospace industry, but were plasma-like conscious entities. Conscious craft were expelled out of the mother ship, while others returned. Continual dock and release. With each digestion and expulsion, the shape of the mother ship morphed. There was an obvious consciousness component at work. I was enchanted. I was hooked. I sensed a similarity to human consciousness.

Questions swirled. Do humans possess an extraterrestrial conscious ability? Is there an extraterrestrial dimension within our consciousness? Is it part of our DNA? Is it integral to our body as well as our mind? If so, what does it do? Can we learn to use it? Manage it? What help is available? The familiar UFO phrase, "we are not alone" was replaced by the possibility that an examination of consciousness might confirm that "we were never alone."

Is our body the mother ship and our consciousness the craft? As though a deck of mental cards reshuffled, my paradigm shifted. All my years of yoga, *tantra*, bodywork, and spiritual discipline opened to a new reality. Was my body the propellant? Was I the zero-point? Was the consciousness I so faithfully nurtured and developed being prepared to launch and re-enter as mother ship? Was Maussan's video simply a display of astral projection on a macro-scale? Was I both the mother and the ship? If so, how many ships could I launch? Did I possess one consciousness or many? Could my consciousness multiply? Could I possibly evolve into a mother ship with hundreds, if not thousands of craft? Were these craft beings showing me the way?

As I began to search for a term to describe the phenomenon, the concept of exoconsciousness emerged. As I integrated consciousness craft knowledge, I intuitively sensed that humans possess an extraterrestrial consciousness, or exoconsciousness, integral to our bodies and our minds. We possess a cosmic consciousness which links us directly to what the ancients called the "star visitors" and we term "extraterrestrials". Human consciousness is directly linked to the cosmos and its inhabitants. We possess a cosmic cord that can be used to travel, communicate, and evolve as intergalactic beings.

What are the Benefits Exoconsciousness?

➤ Exoconsciousness encourages a new relationship to self, other humans, intelligent beings, planet Earth, and the Universe.

➤ Exoconsciousness accelerates mental, physical, emotional, and spiritual development, achieving an integrated, peaceful, healthy, and harmonious state of being.

➤ Exoconsciousness offers humans an unparalleled experience of the vast power and potential of consciousness, strengthening their intuitive, telepathic muscle, and opening their ability to receive and transmit information and energies among multiple dimensions.

➤ Exoconsciousness accesses information and experience of our species extraterrestrial "birthright." Suddenly, we understand who we are, where we are sourced, what we are to be about, and why our development is essential for planet Earth, our galaxy, and the Universe.

➤ Exoconsciousness provides a platform for the integration of technology and consciousness.

➤ Exoconsciousness eases the transition of our species from an Earth-bound to a space-faring race, promoting the entrance of humans into a peaceful, evolved, and universal society.

Each and every master, regardless of the era or place,
heard the call and attained harmony with heaven and earth.
There are many paths leading to the top of Mount Fuji,
but there is only one summit.
Morihei Ueshiba

CHAPTER 1
THE CALL

Life is many calls, one summit. During my life I responded to my heart's call to marry and raise beautiful children. I responded to my mind's call to study and pursue graduate degrees. I responded to my church's call to ordination and service. Calls answered easily and eagerly.

Then a different call sounded. It shuddered, shoved, and smacked. It speared me. During the Holy Week of 1996, there was no ignoring its presence.

In 1992 I moved from Dayton, Ohio to Scottsdale, Arizona with my husband and three of our children. It was a transition of cascading fortuitous openings. Prior to the move, during a visit to Scottsdale, the McDowell Mountain energy burned into my being and its vibration continued to resonate. Our house in Dayton sold to the first buyer, friends offered their Scottsdale home as a base for my husband, and our children delighted in the prospects of a new home out west. All fell into place so that we could dwell in the fire energies of Phoenix.

I did not know that fire energies combust and burn the dross of our being. Four years into life in Scottsdale, I was on fire. Another being awakened and emerged. Now I realize that I chose to combust, resurrect, and reignite. During the process I was stunned and awed.

The shift was dramatic. In 1992 I moved to Scottsdale a wealthy woman, living in a luxurious, art-filled home with my husband and children. After leaving my job as an ecumenical chaplain at a state university in Ohio, in Scottsdale, I chose to devote my now-free-time to writing. I spent my days writing and orienting our children to a new home. My husband flailed. He pursued a real estate development career by day and a growling drinking depression by night. It was not a smooth transition, yet it was where we belonged.

By Holy Week of 1996, I was teetering on the brink of bankruptcy, foreclosure of our home weeks away. I swallowed the sour reality of a defunct writing career, a failed marriage, and the looming prospect of raising adolescent children as a single parent. By Holy Week of 1996 the burn was complete. All that was left were the ashes of Wednesday.

The night of Ash Wednesday I wakened to a loud drumbeat as if a large bird hovered over the house. Wings opened and closed, pulling and pushing a powerful energy field. I opened my eyes, sat up as the bedroom illuminated and watched a large serpent drop from the fireplace and land at the foot of my bed. Telepathically I heard the summons, "You are on a wind current carried to your destination. We want you back. You are ancient." The room filled with spirits—ancient Native American, extraterrestrial, unknown beings.

That night another call summoned me. This time it echoed through my eternity. This time the response would not come as easily or eagerly. This time there was no midwife, no curriculum, no discipline, or doctrine. This time the answer to the call was within.

What happened that night of ashes? Was it a spiritual phenomenon? Was it extraterrestrial contact? Were the pulsing sounds a craft? Were the beings from another dimension? Were they ET or Native American or unknown origin? And what was the serpent?

The imprint of the experience remained, but there was little time to ponder its significance. There was a life to maintain, survival to summon.

Looking for work, I shopped my graduate degree to no avail and landed right where I belonged, selling designer clothing at an upscale department store. My days were surrounded by beauty, interesting customers, and a covey of strong women. My nights were surrounded by angry, insecure, hopeful adolescent children. My body and spirit determined to create a nest for three beautiful, strong eaglets.

Then the door to **Alanon** opened. I sat through my first meeting numb and incredulous, until it was my turn to speak. Dare I give my reality a verbal form in front of strangers? Dare I break the spell of secrecy?

Softly the words formed, exposing veils of my trauma and fright as the wife of an alcoholic. I spoke the familiar story of the endless thunderous nights and the eternal hope of morning. I spoke of holding the energy for another, confident that they would turn around. I spoke of losing my sight, my power, and my mind to a disease that roared endlessly. I spoke of the horror of watching the disease occupy and destroy another's life. And then I dissolved into a sobbing, hysterical heap.

Speaking my truth broke a powerful dam of emotion. Night after night I returned to the meetings, eager to dismantle my fortress. Eager to rid myself of terror, confusion, and disappointment. My words became my strength.

Amid the power of sharing my experience, another foundation crumbled. We lost our home to have another appear. The new condo was small, yet forced us closer. Intimacy was essential. We were a tribe of four—three children and a mother determined to survive and create a future for her offspring.

During those early years together, the memory of sound was hip-hop as my children held the vibration of their generation. The memory of smell was tobacco as they held on to the last vestiges of their father through cigarettes. The memory of texture was a dense dark weave as they chose ways to float through their grief that included drugs and alcohol. The memory of happiness was the ritual of nightly meals together, holiday celebrations with family, and a little church that offered the safety of familiarity. So whether they had partied or rebelled the night before, my children gathered nightly at the dinner table, worshipped on Sunday, and connected with family on holidays.

Born an Evangelical United Brethren and then integrated into United Methodism, it seemed that churches quietly appeared at essential junctures in my life. As a college student traveling in London, I learned of my older brother's death while staying in a Wesley House. After hearing the news, the director calmly took me to the bank, withdrew $600, and put me on a plane home to my brother's funeral.

Now, once again the church calmly took my hand and provided me strength and tradition. The minister had 20 years sobriety. He lived the steps. His massive gentle hands and clear blue eyes echoed discipline, stability, and intellect. His assistant held a familiar vibration of female power, wisdom, and beauty. They became the yin and yang of our support system. They were the voice on the other end of the phone when my children were afraid and I was at work. They were the structure that echoed the promise of a better future.

The approaching calm phase would not have unfolded for our family without their presence in our lives. Fear, instability, panic, and anger did not simply evaporate, we had to be cradled, stroked, and comforted by love and peace, tradition and faith.

Occasionally my son and his friends would skateboard near a sports bar frequented by my soon to be ex-husband. My son's friends would taunt his dad and ask him for quarters for video games. Angry, abandoned, and embarrassed my son would return home withdrawn and aching. One Sunday morning I told the minister of my son's experience and asked what I could do or say to help him. He looked at me and smiled (I call it the sobriety smile—they all have it).

"The only thing you can do to help your son is to Forgive His Father."

And so I forgave his father, and in turn forgave myself, and in turn opened the path for my children to forgive themselves. One key unlocked a hallway of hearts.

A nightmare of resentment, sorrow, and anger ended that Sunday morning. Then the visitations began again. An inter-dimensional guidance of information and energy flowed into my life. Days past with selling clothes, repairing cars, finding the finances to send my daughter to college, and resources to support adolescent spending habits. I lived ordinary days filled with retail customers and anomalous nights filled with curious phenomenon. I had no idea what was happening, only that I did not fear its manifestation.

A solid theological education and a lifetime of study provided clues to the inter-dimensional reality, but little guidance. There was the Bible, the lives of the saints, and philosophers' speculation; but none were similar to these experiences. I was on my own.

Colored **orbs**—red, brown, orange, or white—manifested nightly in my room, hovering in the corner, then whizzing by my head. They squealed like dolphins in a language I somehow comprehended telepathically. They seemed intelligent beings simply checking on me. Arriving, they gently wakened me then whizzed across the room. I felt safe and secure despite their high-pitched squeals, which I decided was laughter-talk.

At night or relaxing in the sun on my patio, voices from what seemed earth inter-dimensional energies would manifest and beckon me. Shifting into their vibration to communicate, I would receive instructions to mentally move my consciousness to a designated destination within the earth, ocean, or space. There, alone or with a group of others, energetic pulses were sent to heal a planetary fracture, or surround an energy event. Other times they pulled me into a space dimension. I now recognize it as an astral plane. There I would work, receive information, communicate, remove energy bodies, gather, and emit light. All these "missions" came naturally, without instruction or rules. I understood and acted.

As the intensity of the phenomenon increased, so did my need to play catch-up. I instinctively knew what I was doing, yet wanted to upgrade my power. This energy was my work, my Dharma, my purpose.

On morning commutes down the Arizona Beeline highway past the Red Mountain I asked for openings and acceleration of my power. I asked that my senses be expanded, that my eyes, ears, nose, mouth, hands, and mind all be given enhanced abilities. Mantra-like day after day I would repeat the request. The answer was unexpected.

It came in the form of a cave. Red Mountain is peppered with caves and from a distance the mountain resembles the shape of a Native American head. Mornings I would watch the sun break creating shadows over the caves, marking their entrances.

At night I entered those caves. Darkness in the desert, free of urban lights, is a vast, bottomless pool. Within the dark I discovered light. At night I closed my eyes and allowed my body to release the physical exhaustion of work and parenting. Sleep came quickly, bringing with it startling images within the caves. The visions were vivid and traumatic, yet somehow, familiar and comforting. I visited, what I now understand to be, a past life.

Body stretched, spinning on a wheel, engulfed in flames, to the rhythm of a rattle, a familiar voice spoke, "We want you back." Echoing the call of Holy Week, it was time to retrace my learning. Time to remember my ancient knowledge.

Contact Experience

Memory of the Holy Week experience lay fallow in my consciousness for a time. Then I discovered UFO, extraterrestrial literature, and the profusion of contact experience recorded by hypnotherapists, psychologists, physicians, and researchers. From the early 1950s through the present, the number of experiencers who witnessed phenomenon linked to extraterrestrials and UFOs has steadily increased.

Extraterrestrial witnesses, who choose a public platform, risk scorn and ridicule. Yet, they also gain affirmation, empathy, and support from a growing contactee community. Alanon taught me the value of public story. Experiencers and contactees who publicly share their experiences provide a platform for healing and connection. An early pioneer in contactee research was John Mack, a Harvard Psychiatry professor. Mack brought personality, practicality, and believability to contactee experience. His sudden death in 2004, silenced a growing audience eager to share their experiences with him.

Yet Mack lives with us through his writings. In *Passport to the Cosmos: Human Transformation and Alien Encounters* he shared the contact experiences of patients who sought him out to understand their anomalous experiences. One after the other, he was able to piece together a holistic description and approach to witness research.

John Mack's research granted my experience the imprimatur of credibility. According to him, contactees report similar phenomenon and sensations including a humming or buzzing sensation, intense light in the room, and strange beings. They also report floating down the hallway, sighting of a UFO, and dreams of being taken to a ship. Some contactees experience a sensation similar to ***sleep paralysis***.

In another spectrum of the contact phenomenon, scientists like Harvard professors Susan Clancy and Richard McNally attribute abduction to simple brain functions. Clancy's book, *Abducted: How People Come to Believe They Were Kidnapped by Aliens*, associates abduction memories to the tendency of traumatized individuals to create false memories with sleep paralysis. In sleep paralysis, disturbing hallucinations are generated by our brains upon waking.

While Clancy's research has come under question by ufology researchers, the scientific study of brain function in anomalous experience holds promise. Humans are more than neurological wiring, yet a holistic understanding of contact requires an understanding of trauma and brain research.

So, did I experience sleep paralysis Holy Week? Perhaps. If the contact had stopped with one experience, then I would readily chalk it up to a case of fried brain circuits. Certainly I was under stress. Certainly I experienced trauma.

But the contact didn't cease. It continued. It occurred during periods when I was awake and conscious. I knew my experience was more than a neurological lapse. Something else was happening and my conscious mind desperately wanted to comprehend it.

Once again John Mack's research provided reassurance. He explained that abductions often occur in homes, or in broad daylight in cars, or surrounded by nature. As my contact continued while sitting on my patio or running errands, I affirmed Mack's belief that abduction experience was not limited to nightly visitation or sleep paralysis.

I was privileged to meet Travis Walton, whose story, *Fire in the Sky,* told of his abduction in the forested high country of Arizona. Travis and his wife are down-to-earth parents and grandparents, eager to tell you about their thriving family along with an occasional mention of travels to Hollywood to make the movie of Travis' abduction. Meeting Travis, hearing him recount his encounter, you feel the truth of this man. His experience was not sleep paralysis.

Like Travis, many experiencers relate the story of moving through walls or windows, to be beamed up through a light shaft into a craft. In the craft they find a sterile environment, sometimes dark and cool. Eventually they are transported to a larger space with curved ceilings, alcoves, and balconies where they meet alien figures busy at computer-like terminals. Frequently, physical examinations or healings occur. These examinations may cause fear and panic. They can also provide reassurance and healing. Cynthia Crawford, a friend who told her story on local television, related how aliens placed her in a tube that generated a vibration. They told her that she was being healed. She experienced little or no fear. Then they departed quickly. Cynthia was back in familiar surroundings healed of her physical illness.

Once experiencers or contactees return, they are never the same. Their consciousness, their emotional, physical, mental, and spiritual life are permanently altered. Their belief system undergoes a radical realignment. Yes, some experiencers simply attribute the experience to being a dream. Others choose to completely forget or deny the encounter. Those who choose conscious memory undergo the most powerful transformations. John Mack terms the transformation "ontological shock." One's former belief that humans are alone in the universe suddenly shifts to a certainty that we are not alone. Newtonian scientific rational theories no longer work. Each contactee manifests an individualized re-entry. They may realign their allegiance to the planet Earth. They may choose to exercise mental abilities such as telepathy and astral travel. They may commit themselves to the survival and evolvement of the human species. Each experiencer designs their personal re-entry.

Through contact, a new level of human development is possible. First the individual must push through the trauma and fear to find acceptance. It takes emotional muscle and spiritual stamina to make the breakthrough. Yet, once one is on the other side, everything changes. Individuals who accept and embrace their contact begin to live in multiple worlds, parallel universes, slipping like a nymph in and out of paradigms. They can move "back" to retrace and clear past lives or into a new present that conjures the warmth and comfort of a cosmic home that harmonizes with their Earth home. Some report the gradual emergence of an alien or star identity alongside their Earth identity. This identity can extend to reunion with cosmic groups or families. The three-dimensional barrier of time and space no longer exists. It is easily traversed with movement into another dimension unbounded and ripe for exploration.

Contactees move beyond Maslow's hierarchical levels. They shift quickly and permanently into willing participants in a loving universe of connectedness with fellow humans and fellow extraterrestrial beings. The psychological term transpersonal takes on new meaning. They participate in a reciprocal human-extraterrestrial interaction that includes communication, travel, and discovery of untapped skill and potentials. The contactee's definition of what it means to be human expands to include abilities once regarded as super-human—telepathy, astral travel, manifestation, and teleportation.

What about those Orbs?

Glowing, plasma-like orb encounters seem to be an initial definable stage of contact. With the advent of digital photography, orbs appear in photos of amateurs and professionals. Some persons even play with orbs. They call them in with telepathic summons and then photograph their atmospheric antics. A family photo can now frame a multi-dimensional gathering of kindred spirits.

My initial encounters with orbs were conscious. Orbs would materialize in my living room and whiz by while I was reading. At night they would awaken me and squeal their desire for nocturnal contact. At times my bedroom felt like an inter-dimensional sleep-over. Often the hour was too late and the visitors too eager to communicate. Eventually, their presence grew so familiar that I sensed when they were ready to make an appearance. It was similar to the feeling that someone was going to call prior to the phone ringing. They would alert me prior to their appearance.

So what are these orbs? I can only speculate. They seem to be intelligent thought forms, perhaps mind projections or energy forms. They are different than ghosts or the spirit of a deceased person. They are connected to extraterrestrial visitation and communication. They are delicate vibrations with a frequency too high to linger in the Earth's atmosphere. Here and gone, they whiz, a momentary intelligent phantom.

Later I discovered that digital photographs were capturing similar orbs and that some crop circle investigators attributed the crop circles' creation to their presence. I learned that some geographical locations such as Hessdalen, Norway, had ongoing, frequent vistas of gathering plasma orbs that attract international teams of researchers.

Digital cameras have a shutter speed of 30-1/8000 per second compared to a 35mm camera with a speed of 30-1/2000 per second. So, digital technology grants us access to a new sliver of visible light. Yet a sliver is just enough. All humans see is a sliver on the familiar science class chart of the electromagnetic spectrum of frequencies. Imagine the electromagnetic spectrum of frequencies as an exotic oriental fan. At one outer most point is the Hertz field of frequencies (power and telephone) and at the other outer point are Gamma Rays. Our visual field is merely a thin slice of the fan, rather insignificant when compared to the entire frequency field. And yet, it is our slice of reality.

The *auric* field surrounding the human body provides a glimpse of the breath of our frequency potential. We have the potential to access more than the sliver of visible light. Healers determined that we have two fields, or separate bands each containing up to seven higher frequencies that surround our physical body. Furthermore, they believe that we have a body for each of these seven frequencies within the two bands. For example, we may have ultra-violet, x-ray, and even a gamma body. If so, then we can learn to recognize and use each of these frequency bodies—determine their different sensations and abilities. Healing with subtle frequencies occurs on these outer frequency levels. It will be discussed later.

Surrounding environmental frequencies affect us as humans. Our physical body is grounded with an earth frequency. Our physical body vibrates with the same frequency as the earth—around 8 Hz. This earth frequency may modulate up and down, yet with each modulation we adjust. According to students of electromagnetic earth changes the Earth's vibratory number will rise as the magnetism of the earth shifts. As goes the earth, so go its people.

The way in is the way out
The way out is the way in
Unknown

CHAPTER 2
INTO THE LABYRINTH

Visions guided me. Shifting into this strange, familiar, yet new reality, I released dependence on books, ritual, and experts. Nightly I entered the same cave—deep and narrow, lit by a small fire. In my visions, I lay by the fire, swaddled tightly in a blanket that covered my body and face. Next to me sat an elder with topaz eyes, deep wisdom facial lines, and long, braided white hair. Against the wall stood a long staff, a stick ringed with changing colors depending on the lesson. Red, blue, yellow, black, white—each color had a lesson. At times he held a mask with vacant eyes, instructing me to focus through the eyes. Beyond the vacant abyss of stare lay meaning. It was my job to allow knowledge to surface from a dark, expansive void. It was my job to allow my consciousness to expand and know.

He assured me, "The physical world will unfold; you must learn to live in the spirit world. You live between worlds. You have a gift, given by creator. You know your gift. It comes from your lineage. It is ancient knowledge buried in your soul."

Bound and silenced in the cave, I became aware of a past life where I had spoken publicly only to be silenced, my tongue cut out, left to die. Bleeding to death, the elder hid me in a cave, away from the community that scorned me. Not ready to hear information, they silenced me. In

13

the cave, I healed, strengthened and learned to communicate without words. Dimensions, sounds, and energies opened. Night after night this same elder who nurtured me in a past life returned to me. Like a father, he flanked me. His brown hands offered me colored sticks to prod my memory. Holding each one, I moved into their color frequency, their field of knowledge and power, rekindling, reawakening.

I devoured his library of colored sticks, until one night, the lessons were complete. He removed the bandages. Unfurled head to toe, I stood in the cave entrance awake, alive, powerful, re-membered. Then, ready to fly, I stepped beyond the bounds of the cave—only to fall deeper into the Earth.

Entrances to the spirit world, the **underworld**, are like tunnels into Earth dimensions—liquefied portals of warm, swirling energy. Long, spiral paths shadowed by spirits loom past the openings. Moist, damp earthen smells filled my nostrils. Winding staircases led to deep azure pools where I dove unafraid. I traveled through whirlpools and tidal waves to narrow openings that led to safe ledges, safe lodges. An unspoken command opened doors of brilliant blue-green rooms, filled with smooth slick stones. These slabs or monuments columned openings lit by brilliant white light—the presence of creation. I moved into the life force of Earth.

On a new channel, night after night, underworld visions continued. One lesson following another, until my soul felt stretched taut. Pulled like an animal skin nailed to the side of a barn, I began slowly resurrecting memory of my childhood in West Virginia. In Arizona, land of ancient Native Americans, I felt the pull of childhood roots of an ancient mountain culture. This West Virginia mountain culture, the land of my birth, coupled human, animal, and Earth.

Pulled taunt by the elder and inner Earth journeys, I tore openings. Childhood memories awakened. Memories flashed of long, leisurely days playing in the hollows of a small West Virginia town. Then the air liquefied, I saw myself as a pony-tailed young girl pulled into the underworld, visiting and exploring. Then I saw myself walking out of the inner earth, up through the tree filled hollow, stepping on to the gravel alley that led to my home.

Memories flooded. My nocturnal travels were not a new experience. As a child, I walked the underworld, the inner Earth, as I did now as an adult. I relearned the path—in and out. The path did not spiral to a high summit, but to a low core—the brilliant white light of creation buried in planet Earth.

The core of the underworld dimension is mythical, magical, and malevolent. Depending on your orientation, it generates fear, awe, familiarity, or excitement. The underworld dwells dimensionally below our feet, recessed deep in the interior of our souls, minds, and bodies. It is accessed by a cord, strengthened by use, tightened by trust. The underworld is our legacy as much as the crust of the earth on which we walk, play, dig, and build. Accessing core dimensions anchors us to the earth, reminding us of our humanity, our choice to enter this dimension as Earth beings. Earth beings, we are invited to step below the surface, where we are given respect, knowledge, and love.

Is it dark? Yes, and sometimes it is brilliantly light. Is it frightening? Yes, and sometimes warm, inviting, beautiful, and fun. Is it evil? Is it the dwelling place of the devil? No, it is an Earth dimension. It is the underworld. Is it here (pointing down)? Yes and no. It is inter-dimensional. It is alive.

Will spirits of the underworld kidnap us and not allow us return? Stories and myths circulate about those who entered this dimension and did not want to return or were held against their will. That is not my experience. The cord of return is always available and easily accessible. Like astral projection, we are corded to dimensions and easily return to our bodies. It's as easy as asking to "go home." Our consciousness knows the way. It is impossible to be lost. It is impossible to be held against our will. We live in an eternal, multi-dimensional Home.

As earthlings, we are privileged children wandering the crust, the thin veneer of the underworld core. The underworld is another dimension of our consciousness. This core of the underworld belongs to a dimension of our consciousness. Fear of the underworld is a myth of crust-dwellers not yet ready to enter. Humans belong to the core. Humans belong to the underworld dimension. We belong to its knowledge and power. We participate in its energy. Awakened, we are invited to share in its bounty.

Religious Roots in the Underworld

Why was I so drawn to the underworld? An intelligent, technologically savvy 21st Century woman infatuated by the underworld—does that make sense? There is a memorable scene in the movie *Sabrina*, where her father accuses Sabrina of reaching for the moon in her infatuation with the son of his employer. Sabrina, smiles and replies, "No, father, the moon is reaching for me."

Sabrina had it right. The underworld was reaching for me and I was responding. Like searching in Wikipedia, a cascade of information links coupled by magical events ensued. One of my friends, a devout Buddhist, invited me to the Phoenix Art Museum opening of *Demonic Divine in Himalayan Art* organized by the Rubin Museum of Art in New York. A delightful, teddy bear Rinpoche gave the invocation at the opening. He compared the wrathful aspect of Himalayan art to a fierce, protective mother. Within her being she holds both compassion and wrath, ever ready to protect her family.

That was it. That was the pull of the underworld. A single mother, responsible for the protection and survival of her family, of course I resonated with the power of the wrathful, protective underworld.

New vistas of the underworld opened as worn out thoughts and attitudes shifted. Being Christian, one of my first beliefs to shift was the story of Jesus' 40 days in the desert, prior to commencing his formal ministry. His wilderness encounter with the devil permeates the consciousness of every student of sermons and Sunday School. In his third (sacred number) desert encounter, the devil takes Jesus to a high mountain, promising him the kingdoms of the world and its splendors, if he will bow down and worship the devil. Jesus refuses and as the story tells, he goes on with his ministry mission.

As I experienced the underworld, questions bubbled. Was Matthew's story of Jesus' encounter with the devil devised to place a mental block in the believer's mind—not just against the devil, but also against accessing the underworld? Was the underworld all that threatening? So far, it was not my experience. Was it either devil or divine? No. It was neither demonic nor divine in my experience. And yet, through my academic training, I understood that religions often dealt with ancient wisdom by usurping or demonizing it. For example, the Roman Catholic Church built their cathedrals and churches over ancient primitive sacred sites, harnessing their power. Some ancient Buddhist art features Lamas, who like the writers of **Gnostic** Gospels, were subject to banishment from the accepted canon of literature. Hebrews weaved story after story to emphasize the demonic aspect of Baal and excluded storytellers who told of another reality.

And yet, I suspected something else was going on. Sometimes wisdom flows easier from another culture. It is easier and less threatening to see details from a distant reality. Within Himalayan art, each mountain community has mountain deities. The curator from the Rubin Museum of Art explained that unless the region was known, it was impossible to identify the regional deities. Like a quilt pattern or a yodel or a dance, regional mountain cultures create a fortress around their wisdom. Wrathful protector spirits dwell in contented mountain anonymity.

It is interesting how Abraham and Moses ascended mountains to communicate with God. Then changing the story, the gospels tell of the devil taking Jesus up the mountain in order to communicate with him. What shifted between the Hebrew culture and the advent of Christianity in respect to mountains? Why did the Hebrew mountain God, through Christian gospels, become identified with the devil? Whatever the motivation, a successful block of the mountain underworld ensued, using story of prejudice and fear.

It is not either/or: Christian vs. Jew, Muslim vs. Christian, Hindu vs. Buddhist. Embraced by the underworld, dichotomies fade. Energies spin in harmony. Like a Russian doll, wisdom is encased in wisdom.

Horseface

Funny how as a child, my father chose to call me horseface. I never understood the reference, didn't own a horse and thought my father funny. Then I consciously entered the underworld, only to meet—you guessed it—horseface. My father was unconsciously giving me a secret message, an ancient Chinese-Taiwanese calling card.

After retiring from full-time ministry, my father became the English-speaking pastor of a Taiwanese congregation in Columbus, Ohio. The assignment blossomed into a mutual love affair. They adored my father's kind, attentive ministry to their English-speaking youth. He and my mother relished the Taiwanese cuisines served communally after services. They shared a beautiful, mutual vibration.

Within the arms of the Taiwanese congregation also lived the Chinese spirit of the underworld. One of the main tourist attractions in Taiwan is the Tungyn Temple of East Hades—the underworld. The temple was built to the primary god or guardian of the underworld, Titsang Wang, King of the Underworld. Horseface, my namesake, was a subsidiary temple deity.

As I traveled through visions, books, and coincidences of the underworld, I began to recognize that not only horses, but also many other animals serve as guardians of the underworld. Pluto—a Disney dog—was a primary Roman guardian of the underworld. It was Pluto who kidnapped Persephone and her mother Ceres, taking them deep into the underworld. Doing so, the season of winter was created. Pluto is commonly regarded as a mythical evil creature—stealing women and children. (That is, until cartoons changed the image.)

Originally Pluto represented wealth as in mining gold and silver. Our ancestors understood that we literally gain wealth by mining the Earth and embracing the underworld. Unfortunately, like many prospectors, spiritual travelers often availed themselves of the riches, only to return home and create scary stories to prevent encroachment. West Virginia's abandoned mine shafts peppered with Danger/No Entry had the same motivation. I can't even imagine the rings of security, fear, and superstition circling African diamond mines. I was quickly learning that despite religious, corporate, political, or spiritual signage, the underworld belongs to each and every human who walks its surface. Once hearts open to the possibility of a wider dimension, animal guides appear. Horses, dogs, wolves, and snakes manifest to lead the traveler. We only need take the reins.

No energy is satisfied remaining in a state of pure unconscious repetitive habit. That is not what energy is about.
John Rappoport

CHAPTER 3
RECALL

One way of comprehending an experience is to become a teacher. The minister at the United Methodist Church offered his study Sunday mornings for a small group to meet. I was to design the curriculum and teach the class. As the nightly visions continued, my body was playing catch-up. Were the visions all in my head?

I was unaware of parallel-heightened experiences in my body. Had I checked out from my body and become oblivious to its changes? How were transformations in my consciousness affecting my body?

Instinctively, I sensed I was becoming top heavy. My mind wanted to ignite my body and I needed to prepare physically for take off.

I chose as a class resource, Carolyn Myss' book, *Anatomy of the Spirit,* integrating Christian and Jewish ritual with the body's **chakra system**. The class was small and the sharing intimate.

Intellectually I learned, experienced and then taught the Hindu 7-based Chakra system. The *root chakra*, signified by the color red, coils like a serpent (there's that creature again) at the base of your spine. It holds the energy of your roots—your family, bloodline, religion, and tribe. The *second chakra* spins from your sexual organs. Seat of your "self," it is the energy center where you experience joy in the physical world as a human body. Its orange energy infuses your sexuality, power, control, and independence. The *third chakra* is your power center, a nuclear reactor just above your navel. Seat of your will, its yellow energy center in your solar plexus thrusts you into the world where you determine who you are, what you want, where you are going, and how you arrive.

Green energy of the *fourth chakra* generates from your heart, infusing you with love and compassion. It is a touchstone that realigns you with others, your world, and yourself. The hidden electrical power of the heart is limitless, boundless, and corded to eternity. Moving up the body to the *fifth chakra,* the throat holds the blue energy of sky and water. Through its communication energy, you speak your truth, connect to others, and transmit and receive information. It demands nothing short of authenticity. As you live your truth, your throat chakra opens to provide clearer transmissions of information in the form of language.

The third eye, in the middle of the brow, is the seat of the *sixth chakra*. It holds the indigo energy of mind. Mental clarity, intuition, wisdom, and intelligence emanate and flow from this portal. Human physical eyes and the spiritual third eye compose a pyramid vortex that opens to the pineal gland. The pineal is the pinecone-shaped gland, the size of a grain of corn. Located in the center of the brain, it secretes melatonin, the hormone of darkness. Many use melatonin as a sleep supplement. This hormone is also known to be a powerful antioxidant with anti-aging properties. The pineal is the seat of what the Egyptians called the light-body. Its power source is a superconductor that can raise your vibration such that you might literally float.

The *seventh, crown chakra* is crystalline violet white and nestles above your head like a crown. As humans, we each possess the headdress of royalty. You possess a halo of light opened through energy of the crown chakra. You wear a thousand-petal lotus opening to receive and transmit information to and from the universe. It connects you with all that is. You are all that is, no more. You are created creator. Through the crown chakra you are one with the great "I am."

Knowledge of these colors, energies and lights felt like a spectacular Cirque de Soliel. I was in the audience, loving the display of knowledge. Clapping ringside with glee at the contortions and possibilities, I was also experiencing emptiness, a not knowing.

While teaching the class, a friend returned from a cruise and gave me an important gift, a small booklet of yoga exercises from his onboard exercise class. The booklet told of a man's journey to Tibet and the lessons he learned about his body and spirit. It promised health and youth. Everything about the gift felt right. I held the instructions to my heart and silently vowed to accept his gift by practicing the positions.

Not one to hesitate when something feels right, I began to practice the exercises. They didn't take long, fifteen or twenty minutes a day. Quickly those exercises became my meditation, my prayer life. Upon awakening, my feet hit the floor, and I began the exercises. Every morning. I was hooked.

Through my exercise ritual, my Sunday morning teachings about energy systems gained the depth and reality. My emptiness of not knowing was filling with realization and wisdom. I was center ring of Cirque de Soliel, no longer relegated to the audience. I had forced myself up, out of the audience, and into the act.

In Alanon rooms I witnessed the physical ravages of the survivors of alcoholism and addictive relationships—cancer, arthritis, and pain. One cannot sit in Alanon and not feel disease and celebrate healing. Trauma, violence, broken promises, and shattered illusions take a toll on the human body. Mine was no different. I had lived years in what one might politely refer to as "extenuating circumstances." I asked that my body be whole and healthy, now I had a key. I chose to unlock my potential.

Wobbly with the first exercise, every morning I began to spin. Twenty-one times, arms extended. Dervish movements rebalanced my depleted system. It seems that whirling moves the electrical system of the brain—right, left, right, left—until a powerful centering occurs. I felt the impact first in my brain. Then realized other systems in my body were also benefiting. Spinning works for me. It feels good. My brain, body, and energy systems love its movement. As I moved through the remaining yoga positions, my body remembered the balance and fusion of untapped energy sources.

Little did I know that as my body grew strong, it also would begin to work again as a vessel of communication. I continued to learn from my body. In constant contact with my physical body, I became conscious of the information and energy it transmits. I trust my body's voice. I heed my body's wisdom. It's simple, once realignment is complete. All realignment requires is discipline and commitment. Easy and effortless.

Over the years the simple breathing and yoga postures have expanded to include additional exercises and extended postures. Energy systems of my body open each morning—my primary and secondary meridians, chakras, and extended auric field. Then my morning intentions are solidified with what may be an ancient Egyptian arm movement that starts at the heart, moves to the base chakra, and flows back up into a beautiful arm extension.

Next, I bless my entire body. The movie, *What the Bleep,* popularized Emoto, Masaru's *The Hidden Messages in Water.* His study and scientific findings resonate for the human body that is primarily water. (Baby's bodies are composed of 78% water and adult bodies vary between 60 to 65% water.) According to Emoto's work, as water is blessed, thanked, and respected, its crystals transform into beautiful clear shapes. Following yoga exercises and intentions, I lie on the floor and move my hands over my body, starting with my stomach. I bless, honor, respect, and thank each cell and molecule, setting the intention of health, beauty, and happiness.

My ritual ends with an exercise given by a wise teacher and healer. She shared the exercise in a class and I immediately resonated and added it to my daily ritual. With this final ritual I blanket my loved ones and myself with love, comfort, protection, and prosperity.

An Alanon survivor, I respect the potency and power of fear. The power of fear overwhelms and blinds the recipient, who then filters all reality through its funnel. The power of fear becomes unconscious as we repetitively practice the reality of its presence. In the midst of my deteriorating marriage, had you asked me if I was afraid or fearful, I would have responded "no". I was so immersed in fear that I could not sense its presence or gauge its effect. Trauma, the side effect of fear, is a strange phenomenon that demands respect and vigilance.

In order to recognize fear, I needed to heal enough to separate from its grasp. Separating from fear required patience and time. Soliciting others to detach from a dangerous situation assumes they are capable of knowing they are in danger. Living in a heightened state of constant fear, one cannot detach. The energy cords are too dense. Release must come by gradually trusting enough to release, resolve, and remove the cords of fear. That's the secret to recovery.

It has been years, yet still I respect the potency of fear and the potential of attaching to its cords. So each morning I end my ritual by standing and swinging my arms, repeating and affirming my safety, security and light, and then move lovingly through each member of my family, my children, grandchildren, and friends. I bless and secure them with love. Next, I drop my arms, jump into the circle of energy I have blessed, and literally rub the intention up my body, beginning at my feet and moving to the top of my head. Then I bend back down to my feet with a deep inhale. I rise with a deep exhale, opening my arms and intentions, blowing them like seeds into the fertile air.

Awakened Serpent

Gradually, my morning ritual evolved into a tantra-style meditation. The visionary serpent that dropped into my Scottsdale bedroom transformed into an energy current that infused my spinal column. The serpent's message "we want you back" and its reference to my being an "ancient spirit" became clear through the daily yoga practice of tantra.

I was drawn to a celibate practice of tantra, an ancient spiritual art of Hindu origin. Tantra practices are an ancient means of connecting physically to the divine source of creation. Once again, as I began my practice, I met with barriers of misinformation and caution. One spiritual maven after the next warned of the dangers and pitfalls of the tantric path. They warned it was a powerful source of energy, easily consuming and addictive. Others claimed that it was nothing more than an excuse for playful, perhaps inappropriate sex under the guise of spirituality. The signage of danger reported that converts were lost; many never returned to a normal life. Then came the final warning. Certainly, never attempt the practice of tantra alone. You need a guru, or teacher who can pave the way.

Like the underworld signage, I decided to ignore the fearful barriers and move forward in the practice of tantra, using my body and my spirit as my lead. Despite the warnings, I chose to incorporate tantra exercises throughout my morning yoga. I wanted to understand the movements, magic and magnificence of my body connecting to my spirit. I instinctively trusted my body to create the right connections for me. It felt right to open my own path. Following my decision to commit to celibate tantra, I've met people active in the couple's tantra community, read books and learned from the "experts". For me, none of these compared with the knowledge that has gradually unfolded within my own body.

The golden truth of bodywork is that we each possess the instruction book. Reading it occurs with movement. After practicing yoga for over 10 years, I attended my first formal yoga class. I explained to the instructor that it was my first class and diligently kept my eye on her form. I was amazed at how easily my body moved into the gentle exercises. When we finished, she turned to me and said, "You're not a beginner. You held the postures, you know the movements." As I thanked her, I silently congratulated my body for its wisdom.

My spine now operates like a tuning fork—opening, closing, and vibrating. Like an antenna, it sends and receives waves of energy and information throughout my body and spirit. My spinal energy is literally my launching pad to inter-dimensional and extra-dimensional portals. An Egyptian painting depicts a pharaoh riding a serpent into the cosmic realm. That is my reality. My spine is the serpent.

Serpent, spinal wisdom exists within the body of each human being. We only need to accept, experience, and trust the energy that coils within our body, literally our "seat" of knowledge. Certainly we can choose to share our energy with a beloved. For me, that has not been my primary motivation. I use my inner serpent to connect to my divine spirit, to travel the heavens and to root deep into the underworld.

Ever since the door slammed on the Serpent in the Garden of Eden, we have been denied our own power, our own sacred gift. To open the gift, there is no need to replant the Garden or indulge in an Atkins diet of apples. We only need to access our inner serpent. Our inner power awakens as we gradually trust the divine serpent within.

Daily Exercise

Benefits of Exercise:

- Unifies body, mind, and spirit
- Expands consciousness through, in, and beyond physical body
- Establishes exoconscious intentions

I highly recommend you develop a daily ritual and commit to its practice. Many successful and productive mystics, athletes, artists, scholars, entrepreneurs, and healers develop personalized daily routines that begin and end with attention to their mind-body-spirit. The following is my morning ritual. I practiced it faithfully for over 11 years. It served me well. Please take what appeals to you then create and customize your ritual.

Step One: Yoga Exercises

I begin my day performing Tibetan Buddhist exercises. The original book I used was lost. Similar books are Peter Kelder's *Ancient Secrets of the Fountain of Youth*, Books 1 and 2, as well as Christopher Kilham's *The Five Tibetans: Five Dynamic Exercises for Health, Energy and Personal Power.* I perform at least five yoga postures.

Over time I integrated and interspersed tantra exercises into the yoga postures. Tantra includes conscious breathing and movement of the spinal energies from my root chakra, up my spine, through the top of my head, and out into universal consciousness.

Step Two: Opening Secondary Chakras

After I perform yoga and tantra exercises, I use my body as a medicine wheel. It just feels right. I rotate north, east, south, and west, pausing at each direction in meditation. Once again, this is simply my method. I find the rotation helps me maintain focus and concentration. The rotation also links me to ancient earth knowledge that is held by Native Americans and Indigenous tribes. Moving through each of the Four Directions, the meditation exercise is as follows.

Standing, I open my secondary meridian system by consciously moving energy through each of my toes, my feet, and up my legs. The energy empties into a "golden" bowl of light in my stomach. Then I repeat the process starting with an awareness of energy pulsing through each of my fingers, into my hands, up my arms, and across my shoulders. Reaching the top of my head, it then pours through the portal at the top of my skull, cascading through my brain and throat. There the energy again separates into three paths at the collarbone. One path moves down my chest, the other paths travel down and across my breasts. All paths finally empty again into the "golden" bowl of light in my stomach. Note: If you have difficulty "feeling" energy in your body, imagine holding a soft cloth soaked in warm water and gently moving the cloth over your body parts. Soon your mind will easily sense your body's energy without the cloth.

Step Three: Opening Primary Chakra System

After opening my secondary meridian system, I become conscious of my primary chakra system. Once again I use movement through the Four Directions for each chakra. Beginning between my legs, I open an energy system between my calves and lower legs, then my root chakra and gradually move up my body (refer to the chakra description in Chapter Three) until I open my seventh chakra hovering at the top of my head. As I become aware of each chakra, I concentrate on feeling its energy and thank it. As I thank each chakra energy, I maintain focus and keep my mind from wandering.

Moving out from the seventh chakra, I become conscious of my **aura**. A classic text on energy healing is *Light Emerging: The Journey of Personal Healing,* by Barbara Ann Brennan. According to Brennan we possess 7 auric fields that surround our physical bodies. I consciously move energy through these fields.

Step Four: Setting Intentions. Prayer Postures

I complete the energy openings, and then set my intentions for the day. I refine my intentions such that I simply repeat them, out loud, each morning. Intentions are simply "I am…" statements. For example, "I am loving, kind, and compassionate." As I repeat the affirmations I also do a movement. Once again, it just came to me. As I repeat affirmations, I fold my hands, intertwining my fingers, in a prayer position. First they lie on my collarbone, under my throat, and then slide down the front of my body to my pelvic bone. At the pelvic bone, my hands separate, rise up either side of my body, and touch my shoulders. Then both hands rejoin and are placed over my breastbone, where I pat or thump. (At this point it is similar to a thymus thump, where the thymus gland is stimulated.) Then both arms extend straight out from my body, palms up. Finally, my arms are lifted gently such that each forms a C-Shape on either side of my head. This prayer posture feels as if I am Venus standing within my sacred shell. My granddaughter sleeps on her back in this position. It is an ancient sacred posture.

Step Five: Blessing my Body: Cellular Exercise

For the next exercise, I recline on the floor and consciously bless, thank, honor, and love each part of my body, back and front. This ritual uses Emoto's water blessing. I begin by lying on my back and blessing my stomach, rubbing it and repeating: "I love you. I bless you. I honor you." You can create your own affirmation. As I repeat the affirmation

I imagine my cells filling with health and light. Next, I bless my chest, throat, head, arms, and fingers. I bend down and bless my legs and toes. Then I stand and repeat the affirmations on my backside. I begin with my shoulder blades, lower back, and buttocks. To bless my spine, I position the index fingers of both hands so that they touch and then separate. I allow one hand to move up and one hand to move down my spine.

Step Six: Protected and Provided

I complete the morning ritual by surrounding myself with safety, love, and protection. I move my prayer out to my circle of family and friends, holding an image of love for each of them.

Daily dedication to conscious awareness of moving energy through your body opens a new relationship with yourself. Western philosophy, theology, and religion advocates a separation of the "spirit and the flesh." This separation permits the acceleration of the physical sciences and objective oriented research. Our Western culture benefited from this historical separation. Yet, now it is time to reorient back to an integration of body, mind, and spirit. Quantum physics accelerates the integration, as does the adoption of Eastern philosophy and religion. Mainstream access to the Gnostic Gospels promotes integration of body and spirit in Christianity as Kabbala studies reorient and enliven the Hebrew tradition. Or as the classic wedding ritual states: "that which God has brought together let no one separate." Birthed from our divine source, we are wedded to our bodies at birth. While alive, let no one separate us.

The first duty of love is to listen.
Paul Tillich

Chapter 4
Medium Messages

My body opened like a string of Tibetan prayer flags, pulsing in the mountain wind. Colors unfurled and frequencies shifted through my energy centers. As I experienced commuting down the mystical Beeline Highway, when you ask, power centers release as senses expanded.

As this unfolds you begin to feel sound, taste sight, and smell texture. Body wisdom is found through experience. Your senses, like your mind, possess multi-faceted energy receptors. They pick up frequencies in various states. Your mantra-like request for wisdom will be answered.

For a time, I luxuriated in a field of possibilities. I was home in other dimensions. Then daily rituals guided me easily through other life changing events. My daughter left for college and my heart filled with anticipation and loss. My husband's daughter returned from living in Spain and reunited with us, eager to salve father loss with family. Another daughter, fraught with instability and indecision, transferred from one high school to the next, committing finally on a commute to her former Scottsdale neighborhood district. My son continued his search to recover from a loss that was beyond the bounds of a junior high mind and heart. Amid this, I changed jobs. I was offered a position in public relations at a large technical high school, again providing a morning commute down the Beeline highway.

My children were like vulnerable animals, burrowing one hole after the next, in search of the soft soil of comfort and peace. My daughter who returned from Spain was living in her mother's basement apartment with her two children. She laughingly called her room, her "womb." That was where we all longed to be—in the womb of the mother. Only now, she and I were the mothers.

Perhaps we all needed the Great Mother's womb. Or we needed our mother's womb. Or we needed to rediscover the female power granted all women. That was the power I felt emerging within me. The ancient female energy of Ruth, Sarah, Rebecca, Mother Mary, Magdalene, Quan Yin, Ishtar, and Inanna.

During an ice-breaker, a friend taped a sign on my back. We were to meet one another and guess the identity on our back. I was stunned to realize that my friend saw me as Mother Theresa. I felt an invisible finger poke my heart, repeating, "Yes. Mother, yes Mother, yes Mother." My obvious identity hidden from my conscious mind.

As I tapped female mother energies, my psychic abilities heightened. At times I felt like the oracle at Delphi. Warnings or premonitions would blurt out. One evening I walked into a friend's house, told him that his colleague was going to die and that he needed to prepare. I didn't have the knowledge prior to visiting him; it simply poured out. I remember setting down a bag of groceries I had bought for dinner and with that motion, the premonition came forth. Weeks later his colleague died in an accident.

Once premonitions came to fruition, I struggled as all psychics do, with the frightening mixture of guilt, shame, power, awe, and intrigue. The power element was perhaps the most lethal. Instinctively, I felt I could easily lose myself in the power. Fortunately my gift came at a time when my plate was full and there was little time to contemplate the possible ramifications of knowing the future. Casinos, telephone psychics, card readings, and crystal balls lacked appeal. I had a family to tend, bills to pay. Furthermore, I had the onus of religion shadowing me. Even on the cusp of the 21st Century, churches, albeit liberal and intellectual, frowned on psychic ability.

I knew ancient Hebrew leaders did not hesitate to consult oracles prior to battle and that prophets (all men) were respected. Yet, none of these biblical stories mattered. The lingering religious psychic taboo was cold, silent, and real. Don't know too much. Don't say too much. Keep a low profile.

Yet, like most taboos, when questioned and confronted it faded. Most religions have no idea of the source of the psychic taboo. Like a prejudice or a dysfunctional habit, it blindly swirls through generation after generation. And as long as we rarely relate to a handicapped, person of color, homosexual, or a psychic—there is no need to question our assumptions.

Silence holds primal power. It defines reality by exclusion. The vacuum created by silence moves underground, it does not disappear. As my psychic powers increased, I quietly joined the underground. I gave myself permission to tap underground streams and gently wade deeper and deeper toward the headwaters.

As I submerged deeper into my subconscious, the rules changed. A new playing field emerged. I needed to make snap decisions. Yes or no. Accept or reject. Easy. Just choose. No time to wait. You are in the now.

A challenging snap judgment came during a four-day educational seminar where the school's assistant principal sat next to me. I knew her professionally; we had perhaps all of a two-minute conversation prior to the seminar. And, there was scant conversation during the seminar. I was new at the school and financially vulnerable. I needed this job to support my family and I was not going to jeopardize our security. I kept my wit, intellect and psychic ability under wraps. Underground.

And there it stayed, bound, and silenced, until the second day of the seminar. The principal sat on my right at a large table of eight participants who were respectively nodding off, checking their electronic devices and stretching in uncomfortable chairs. Suddenly behind the principal's shoulder an ethereal form manifested. It was a female form—soft, round, and assertive. It demanded to speak to the principal. "Tell her I am here. I need to talk to her. Tell her. Right now. Tell her."

I tried to ignore the presence. There was no way I was going to tell the principal that an invisible presence wanted to talk to her. No way. She would think I was loony. Worst-case scenario, I would lose my job over my outburst and then what would I do? What would my children do? Fear felt like a soiled cloth stuffed in my mouth, choking off my speech.

This was a contest of wills and the presence was not giving up. She refused to leave. She demanded to communicate. Then as her presence enlivened, I began to trust her, even like her. Finally I decided, why not?

During an auspicious break, the presence waited for me. I began diplomatically. But I began. I touched the principal on her arm and looked into her eyes. "I don't know if you believe in spirits, but a large female spirit is behind you and wants to communicate."

Her eyes widened, but she didn't laugh or shy from the encounter. "Who is she?"

"I'm not sure. I'll describe her and maybe you will recognize her. Perhaps she is a relative, a female relative who has passed over. A grandmother, an aunt, a family friend."

And so the tentative dialogue began. I didn't know what I was doing, but the presence obviously did. She communicated telepathically to me and through visions and word thought forms showed me what she looked like, helping the principal to recognize her.

During the break, the two of us sat at the table of eight as others around us disappeared. After numerous descriptions—braided hair, round figure, strong arms dusted with flour, print dress—the principal determined that the presence was her Swedish grandmother. She had died when the principal was a small child.

Presences like to give endearing messages. I was given an image of the grandmother standing in a kitchen wearing an apron. Her hand would go into her apron pocket and give something to the principal as a young child. Again and again she repeated the act. I relayed the image. "I see your grandmother going into her apron pocket and giving you something, maybe a toy or a candy?"

The principal couldn't recall. Then suddenly she cried. "Yes, it is my grandmother! She was always pulling tissues from her apron pocket and wiping my nose, face, and hands. Yes, it is my grandmother!"

My interpretation of toys or candy clouded the communication. I quickly learned to limit my input and stick to simple acts transmitted. The meaning would be determined by the recipient.

The presence continued to relay messages to her granddaughter. She told the principal that she was moving into a time of transition. It would be a long transition. Eventually she would relocate near the ocean where she would be happy. The presence reassured her granddaughter that she would never leave her side. Her love was assured.

After the reading, the principal and I rarely spoke again of the encounter. Months later, she left her job at the school, to dedicate the summer to completing her doctorate and look for a new job. Summer turned to fall. The doctorate was complete, but there was no sign of employment. Finally, the following summer, a position opened on Long Island and she relocated to the ocean, just as her grandmother predicted.

As a medium, presences seem to manifest and communicate when people are ready to move through important transitions. Perhaps spirits are granted a special dispensation to communicate to those they love. Perhaps they are always there and a time of transition focuses their energy. I have no way of knowing how or why they appear to communicate. The phenomenon exists and I chose to participate by communicating what I see, hear, feel, smell, touch, and know. When clarity is not there for the recipient, then I wait. And I wait.

Sometimes I wait for months until the message for a loved one is understood. A friend was looking for her deceased mother's wedding ring and we were discussing it over lunch. Whoosh, in came her mother and communicated that the ring was in a brown purse.

My friend accepted the communication. At subsequent meetings, we discussed the lost ring, until we lost interest. Then, months later, she laughingly told me that while cleaning her bedroom she found an old brown purse belonging to her mother. Almost ready to discard it at Goodwill, she opened it and felt through the pockets. There was her mother's wedding ring, waiting to be found.

Not all messages are easily communicated. Transferring from public relations to career development at the high school, I was assigned a new supervisor. She was intelligent and competent, with a strong background in counseling and education. If there was a job to be done, she was the one to take the reins, a natural leader. A clear-cut communicator, goals and objectives were her primary focus. I liked her blunt, authoritative style. She was hammer and heart.

She walked a daily path by my office. Each time she passed I felt her energy. I knew she was sick. I felt it so strongly that I confided in a co-worker. I just could not hold in the knowledge. The energy was too strong.

Late one afternoon, the supervisor came into my office to discuss some minor details. She sat in a chair that faced a blank white wall. I liked the wall because I could easily see presences manifest and energies materialize. It was a blank slate. I would talk to the person across from me and simultaneously, on another level, read their energies and the presences surrounding them.

During our conversation an older man materialized behind my supervisor. He politely asked to communicate with her. Once again I hesitated. This was my supervisor. Yes, I knew she was sick, but she reviewed my work. An old familiar fear crept into the room, but didn't stay long. My desire to bring health, peace, and happiness to my supervisor was stronger than an old, decrepit fear.

I explained to her that a presence was behind her. At first she was positive that it was her father, whom she loved. But no, the description did not match. She went through one male family member after the next. None matched. Who was this tall, thin, intellectual man with refined bearing, wearing a starched white shirt? As her confusion grew, he tried another route. He kept handing her a pair of eyeglasses. Again and again he motioned to her—take the eyeglasses. Was he asking her to see? Was he asking me to see?

It was late Friday afternoon when the session ended. She and I were both tired and frustrated. I was depleted, but I knew the answer would come in time. Something would trigger her memory.

Monday morning she hustled into my office, bursting with enthusiasm. Over the weekend, reorganizing her desk at home, she came across a pair of eyeglasses given to her by a dear colleague, a school superintendent back in Iowa. The superintendent and his wife were close friends. Some time ago, he had died, leaving his wife. Amazingly, my supervisor and her husband were planning a trip back to Iowa and had arranged to meet with his wife. Her health was failing and it might be their last visit. She professed her adoration for the superintendent and spoke of how she cherished his eyeglasses. Now she cherished his presence in her life and the guidance he offered her from the other side.

Weeks later my supervisor was diagnosed with a fast-growing breast tumor. She triumphed through two surgeries, chemo, radiation, hair loss, wigs, and baseball caps. She triumphed and her vision shifted. New eyes opened. Sight restored.

Practicing as a medium is audacious. It is an audaciously loving act to stand in the mid-point between worlds and communicate. Talk simply and transfer information. So simple. So easy.

Driving down the magical Beeline Highway, bending my body like a supple limb, releasing my consciousness to travel beyond my physical reality, I made the conscious choice to become who I am. I made the conscious choice to move forward, stay in the present, and allow my being to unfold. I made the commitment to walk among worlds. As a theological student I loved Paul Tillich's definition of God as the "ground of being." I was opening to new ways of being and I was grounded in life. The divine source of God was experienced as eternally opening and absolutely relevant.

Magdalene

As my mothering role intensified, I searched for sources of strength. Except for Mother Mary, Western Christianity was somewhat void of female role models. Like an avid archeologist, I dug until I uncovered Mary Magdalene, a female spirit, long buried. Through her I gained wisdom and strength. She became my mother figure. I read all the Gnostic texts of her ministry and relationship with Jesus' family and community. I learned of her possible Hebrew heritage from the Tribe of Benjamin, which created a strong political-priestly tie with Jesus' lineage from the Tribe of David.

Magdalene was my kind of woman—intelligent, beautiful, practical, connected, loving, and comfortable with power. Through Magdalene, I learned the ancient power of numbers.

Numbers are an ancient metaphysical science. The simplicity of numbers reveals hidden meanings and dimensional portals. Understanding the symbolism of numbers opens pathways of consciousness. When we identify with the ancient symbolism of numbers, we gain a deeper conscious comprehension of reality. Of course, the search for numerical meaning can become compulsive with continual counting and re-ordering. With that in mind, I chose to keep it "light."

Multiple methods of reading numbers exist. Some practitioners use name and birth date numerology to determine one's purpose and personality. **Coaches** and therapists use numerology to gain additional information regarding their clients. Numerology provides a quicker assessment than the Myers-Briggs or psychological profiles. Numerology is a different type of crystal ball.

In the art of sacred numbers, each number has an inherent meaning. Each alphabet letter (Hebrew, Greek, and English) has a designated number. There are charts listing letters correlated with numbers. When letters combine into words, the created number has a sum meaning. One technique is to add two digit numbers to gain one number. For example, the number 31 is also 3+1=4. So number 31 is also number 4.

Some biblical scholars search ancient texts, adding and ordering letters as numbers, linking words to reveal clues to our future and our past. Computers accelerated the process, and with it, the number of predictions. For example, take the word "fishes." The fish is a recognized early Christian symbol, or bumper sticker. The Jesus community was "fishers of men." In Greek the word "fish" adds up to 1224. Then numerologists begin to not only add, but to divide. 1224 is equal to

153 X 8. This then leads the numerologist to the sacred number of both 8 and 153.

According to Will Henry in his book *The Illuminator,* the Magdalene's number was 153. Mary Magdalene was revered as "Fish Goddess" in her religious community.

Ancient Jewish **Kabbalah** knowledge was also based on the meaning of numbers. Kabbalah mysticism was regarded as the knowledge "under" the Torah. In this system, numbers were perceived as representing access to structural elements of the universe. Understand the numbers and you understand universal structure. Pretty awesome. Then of course historically, awesome knowledge had to be protected. Only men (married men) were permitted access to this knowledge. That was until Kabbalah went Hollywood and the secret was out and about, infiltrating our culture. With Madonna's Kabbalah conversion, gone are the good old days of secrecy, elitism, and power plays—locked doors and gatherings of the chosen. In the end, it did not matter how much secrecy veiled the art of numbers, as humans we have access to its storehouse of knowledge. We can either expend our energy, angry about historical elitism and past abuses, or learn the art of numbers and use it for our own transformation.

According to Margaret Starbird, author of seminal Magdalene books, the Magdalene mystery was grounded in numbers. Women intuitively practiced the art of numbers. (Well…so, maybe that's why the men needed Kabbalah classes?) Magdalene was known through numbers. According to Starbird, in her book, *Magdalene's Lost Legacy: Symbolic Numbers and the Sacred Union in Christianity,* Magdalene's number ("the Magdalene") was 153. This number 153, as we have seen, was also linked to the fish symbol which is the shape formed by the circumference of two circles moving through one another's centers. This shape is the vesica pisces. It was also known as the doorway to life.

With the sacred number of 153, Mary was acknowledged as the "Fish Goddess" or the New Eve.

Every person possesses a number identity that unlocks their metaphysical and sacred being. You possess a frequency that aligns you with certain numbers. For example, your birth date gives information about you. My birth date is filled with the numbers 6 and 9. Biologically I had 3 children. The number 12 is also significant to me. I was born at 12:24. So, 3, 6, 9, and 12 are my primary numbers. Of course, I identify with The Magdalene, her numbers 153 also add to the number 9. She was the "Fish Goddess" and my maiden name was Fisher. I belong to the Fish tribe.

Three of my children were born on the 28th, so their numbers are 10, or 1. Look around and be aware of the numbers that identify you and your family. This ancient art is not just about learning the meaning of Jesus or the Magdalene. It is about you. The identification and meaning of your numbers will open doors. Your numbers are like an access code to a storehouse of ancient knowledge. This lifetime you can open and use its riches. So, learn your numbers, become conscious of their symbolic meaning and access their sacred information. It's yours.

Our destiny is the stars.
Aerospace executive
Our legacy is the stars.
My response

CHAPTER 5
HOLDING SPACE

Ineffective beliefs disappear. Acting on a commitment to enter multi-dimensional realities as a healer, psychic, or medium realigns foundational beliefs and assumptions. Outmoded judgments based on invalid or incorrect information are discarded. New belief systems form. Learning to suspend judgment during the realignment process was a foundational lesson. Suspending judgment requires holding yourself and others in compassion with an open heart. I had no idea of the boundaries I would cross and the understanding I would gain, simply by suspending judgment.

Suspending judgment is a tough hurdle for those of us indoctrinated into a religious community. An essential mission of religion is to bind society with doctrine, rules, and obedience. Suspending judgment was a huge leap for me as a seminary graduate, ordained and committed to the life of the church. It was a leap I chose to take.

Experiences were unfolding in my life I wanted to embrace. Many of them did not fit with mainline Protestant religion. I began to call them "spiritual" experiences. I saw myself as "spiritual," having an "awakening." My classic 40 days in the desert was lasting months and years.

Now, years into my journey, I acknowledge using "spiritual" as a way to distinguish myself. I needed safe, familiar terminology to shed thought forms and energies I no longer wanted or needed. Once I separated the duality of religion and spirituality, the core reality came into view. Both religion and spirituality are mirror images of me. Am I religious? Yes. Am I spiritual? Yes. There is less need to define. Both play a role in human development. Religious roots provide structure. Religion is the vessel that holds doctrine, ritual, discipline, text, and community. Religion provides a structure for spiritual work. Spiritual work is individual and experiential. I chose to honor my religious roots, yet move beyond religious boundaries in my spiritual journey.

Without a text, doctrine, or teacher, my daily disciplines proved necessary anchors. As my former intellectual, biblical, and authoritarian foundation shifted; my personal discipline strengthened. Personal discipline filled the void, quickly and easily. Yet, for a long time, the back and forth of questioning and assessment of my former beliefs held sway.

Like a deserted lover, I periodically returned to the old ways. Corresponding with a professor friend, I re-read theologians and philosophers like Paul Tillich and Karl Jaspers only to wonder how these academics could understand transcendence without experience. Intellectual, mental concepts were not enough. I re-read Bible stories, gritting my teeth through the violence and purposeful political framing. Story and description were not enough.

Enough reading! I wanted to experience transcendence. Not someone else's transcendence—mine. I came to a certainty. My physical body moved inter-dimensionally as a super-conductor. Like high-spun gold I expelled gravity and experienced lift off. Ancient Israelites traveled with an ark that promoted the same experience. The messiah, a priest king born in Bethlehem, "house of bread," tells of a people fed manna of gold that was transformed into a powdery cake. They ate the bread to reunite inter-dimensionally. It all had to do with becoming a light body. My Egyptian and Hebrew religious legacy practiced inter-dimensional travel. Certainly I could also access their methods. These methods were not lost, they were simply forgotten.

I connected ancient stories with quantum physics. Our body operates as a fuel cell, with the potential for zero-point energy. We expel gravity. We live on a sub-atomic level, a being of energy and information in a void of all possible states of energy and information. On an intellectual level, I was unable to completely comprehend quantum science or the ancient stories, but I sensed an experiential reality.

As humans, we possess a DNA connection to inter-dimensional abilities and quantum information. Our legacy is the stars. We are simultaneously earthling and inter-dimensional, inter-galactic being. If we allow our body to lead us, dropping the reins of our mind and the energy of others that pulls our heart, then realities easily shift. The forgotten is re-membered.

My journey did not follow a logical trajectory from point A to point B. It wound like a spiral through unknown and at times uninviting territory. Still, I suspended judgment. First I experienced, and then, acceptance followed.

Interesting beings manifested on my path to experience transcendence. Very interesting creatures. I believe the animal and plant worlds transmit information. I chose to listen to their messages. During the 2004 Indonesian tsunami, animals fled first. Scientists are studying animal's sensitivity to earthquakes.

Beyond their innate sensitivities, animals communicate wisdom and information. Snakes curl in our path encouraging us to shed yet another skin and live in a new reality. Lizards change colors and teach us when it is time to detach, drop our tails, and grow another. Spiders remind us to weave new insights into our existing web of knowledge. Birds bring wisdom by flying in certain directions, in numbered flocks, dropping feathers for us to treasure. Coyote warns of a trickster, a funhouse of mirrors. Coyote reminds us all is appearance.

The morning before my position was terminated at the high school, I opened the back door to let my cat out and was greeted by a dead bird. On my way to work a coyote wandered lazily in front of my car. There was no need for humans to deliver the message; animals spoke—death by trickster.

Pigs remind us of family, and the need to circle, protect, provide, and love each member. They always travel in families and rarely separate. After my daughter's wedding, a tribe of wild javelina wandered into the photo session. Their cumbersome presence reminded us how precious we are to one another—the unborn baby carried by my bridesmaid daughter, family who traveled great distances, the new acquaintance of my son-in-law's family, and friends of long-trusted heart connection.

Scorpions foretell transformation. I live in the desert on soil amenable to birthing scorpions. It is not unusual to see them posed, stinger erect, on my floor or ceiling. Tiny newborns wiggle through screened openings. Every time I confront scorpion, I remember they carry a message of change. They signal the advent of new information or experiences that will carry me to my next step.

What I did not expect were vivid visions of scorpions. One evening I was awakened by the thud of a visionary creature on the bottom of my bed. I sat up and encountered a massive two-foot scorpion staring at me. I caught my breath before I shrieked. I knew it was a vision, and yet it was so real. My son was out with his friends and I was alone in the house. As the scorpion disappeared, I threw back the covers and ran into the living room to reorient myself. I regulated my breathing. I was okay.

Several hours later my son returned. He didn't keep his usual routine of coming in to tell me he was home. I waited and listened through our thin condo walls while he went through slow motions of preparing for bed. I sensed something amiss in his rhythm. And yet, I felt the need to wait.

Finally, I knocked and entered his room. He was sitting on the edge of his bed, pale and blinking back tears. "Mom, my friend's dead. She died tonight in a car wreck." His eyes were pools of deep sorrow and shock. His friend was a beautiful young girl, a close friend of my son. She was a sprite, full of love and laughter.

Having lost a brother and a stepson to quick, traumatic death with no "goodbyes", I knew the sorrowful, vulnerable time awaiting my son and his friends. They all were shoved across the threshold of change when death grasped their friend, Ashley. The scorpion's size was simply my "wakeup" call to understand the magnitude of my son's transformation and my participation in this traumatic death.

Trusting the vision of the scorpion on that fateful night opened the door for me to trust a parade of visions that later manifested. Like living creatures, animal visions transmit important messages—where we need to go, when, and with whom. They send up a flare to light our way, when it's our time.

Visions break through your boundary of time and space. Ancient, native cultures summon visions on a conscious level with ritual. It is my experience that simply melting into your subconscious realm is the most effective means of connecting with visions. In our modern environment, we are bombarded by electro-magnetic waves—television, radio, computers—all creating static in our conscious mind. It takes discipline to turn away, find silence, and access the gap where your subconscious dwells.

In dreamtime, during sleep, your subconscious switches on. While listening to soothing music, walking in nature, meditating, or singing, your subconscious switches on. Numerous paths lead into the subconscious. Exploring venues is fun. You simply need to commit to one path that works, then use it daily. Walking your path allows energies from other dimensions to openly communicate. Sometimes the communication is otherworldly and magnificent.

One evening, a friend and I arrived late for a concert. The ticket office was closed, but the usher let us sit in the balcony for the remainder of the concert. It featured a choir—voices trained to hold harmonies so perfect they seemed to hover like geometric symbols in the air. I sat enraptured by the sound. It was like nothing I had ever heard. My senses opened and something shifted within me.

Returning home, I slept soundly for a few hours, then woke with a start. Something or someone was in my room. I felt a soft light magnify slowly across the room. Then, as though focusing a camera lens, an angelic presence stood facing me. She was well over 7 feet, if not 8 feet tall. Her body shimmered with light, like a rainbow of mother of pearl. I was stunned by the sheer mass of her presence. She felt kind and loving, yet massive.

Then she spoke, telepathically. She told me that her name was Helen. I remember being amused at the fact that she had such a name. An angel with a name—not Gabriel, Uriel, or Mary—mine was named Helen. At least it sounded like Helen. She told me that she was here to help me and that I had work to do. She told me that she would always be available.

Then my heart began to race, as her presence grew even more large and luminous. My physical body responded in fear. I kept my wits about me and thanked her for coming. I even asked her to turn down her volume next time. She frightened me. She agreed, shimmering like laughter. Then she evaporated, leaving all but her lingering energy and a vivid memory.

The evening's harmonics opened my being to receive her presence. Those harmonics are termed "music of the gods." Our religious tradition cradles the voices of celestial music—choirs, hymns, chants, and pipe organs. Western religious services usually center on the homily or sermon, the power of the word. Yet, music provides the musical portal to transcendence.

Years ago I traveled with my family to a church in Clarksburg, West Virginia where our father had been pastor. My father's aging frame was bent. We discovered later that he had an undiagnosed broken hip. Yet that day, his stature in that religious community was strong and steadfast. By his side, my mother was beautiful—coiffed grey hair, quiet smile, snapping brown eyes. The Sunday morning service honored their presence in the history of that church. The sermon was delivered by a man who rivaled Swaggart, Graham, and Jakes. Then the music began. A modest choir gathered in front of the altar. A cappella, united by one blow of the pitch pipe. Voices merged. Harmonics blended; frequencies rose and fell like waves over the congregation. Song after song mesmerized me. The choir was no longer human; they were voices. The collective sound of eternity. They created music of the gods. Hymns fell like a soft angelic garment, draping over me and my family—blessing us, connecting us, re-minding us of why we chose to gather again in that space after years apart. Hymns re-minding us of other dimensions we share. Hymns re-minding us of accessible portals of **consciousness** that link us to other dimensions. Music and sound are frequencies we travel. Sound functions like an undulating vibrating serpent that we ride into altered states where we connect with new realities and dimensions.

Exercise: Holding a Space

Benefits of Exercise:

- Suspension of judgment
- Becoming an empty vessel ready to receive knowledge

A classic coaching technique involves learning to "hold a space" empty, free of judgment. Life coaches assist individuals seeking a new path. In a coaching relationship, you are able to clarify who you are and where you want to go. You develop detailed goals, objectives, and tasks that lead to success. Coaches accompany others on their inner and outer journey. Coaches work similar to shamans. Coaches contract to walk with others through multiple dimensions that comprise another's spiritual, emotional, mental, physical, and professional journey. An effective way to accompany someone is to remain free of judgment.

Free of judgment. Easier said than done. Students are rewarded for being critical. Acculturated through education, religion, politics, and the media to make snap judgments, it is difficult to disconnect old neural pathways that want to form judgment. It is difficult, yet not impossible.

Through suspension of judgment in the coaching relationship, you are free to embark on a consciousness safari. Like travel to a foreign country, you learn new rules of behavior, see through new eyes, taste new food, and hear new sounds. Old baggage, over packed, over allowable limits, only delays the trip.

So how do you suspend judgment? You simply choose to enter into a state of suspension. If you get lost or confused, and old judgmental thought patterns push into your consciousness--simply fake it. Remind yourself that you are in a state of suspended judgment.

Keep your mouth shut. Turn off the talk. Turn off the analysis. Turn off your sensory dial. Silence the judgment. Allow it to depart. And if it will not leave, then simply pretend it is gone. Outrageously simple, and it works.

As you suspend judgment, you begin to have encounters—with animals, visions, sounds, intelligent beings. Like a butterfly garden, the nectar is silent, suspended judgment. In a garden of suspended judgment--beings appear, messages sound.

What we think as time/space…is a relative thing.
Our appearance, reality and identity are relative and different according
to the relative point of view.
Einstein describes something known in all the worlds' spiritual and
magical traditions—the identity, reality, and location of the human being
is something relative.
R.J. Stewart

CHAPTER 6
BEYOND THE SPACE-TIME
CONTINUUM: WHERE AM I?

Veins of coal run through West Virginia. Men and women enter elevators that drop into the underground, the underworld. My ancestors, German-Scot-Irish, were independent souls who settled West Virginia and mined those veins. Their stubborn independence roots them to the land and the underground long after it is financially or physically viable. What force keeps them living in poverty above abandoned mines? What secrets do the hills and hollows keep?

In Arizona, Native American reservations are portals to other worlds. Underworld creatures inhabit these portals. These creatures are painted in story and pottery—serpent, spider, corn-mother, lizard.

In West Virginia, backwoods communities and generations of close families secure the portals to other worlds. Underworlds inhabited by creatures of story, song, quilt, and craft.

As an adolescent, I recall sitting in a junior high gymnasium in Buckhannon, West Virginia, eating a brown bag lunch on the bleachers. Every school has an industrial smell, probably sanitizing solvents.

Whatever it is, it infiltrates your nose memory during childhood. The school smell is stimulated by pervasive, lifeless, institutional green paint. This school had a particularly pungent smell—rich, fetid, earthy. Gymnasium sweat mingled with childhood lunch aromas. It was a consolidated school system and some of my classmates walked miles out of the mountains to catch a bus, only to start another lengthy journey to school. They were paid a penny a mile to walk to catch the bus.

Next to me, on the bleachers, sat a young girl who rode a school bus home to another world deep within the mountains. Our school was in a small college town that offered planned activities for teenagers she never experienced. Every afternoon her bus crossed the town limits and she entered the foreign space of mountain culture.

During lunch, she related how her mother encountered a snake prior to her brother's birth. Walking into the barn, a snake coiled in front of her and rose to strike. Belly full with child, she ran safely back to the house. When her brother came into the world with a large serpentine birth mark their family and community understood the importance. Her brother was marked. Her eyes widened as she repeated his fate. Her brother was marked.

I did not understand marking. I did not understand mountain life. I did not understand stories of carrying a rifle through the woods on a Friday night to go 'coon hunting. It was more than my adolescent mind could fathom. Yet, her endless stories struck a cord in me. She knew something I knew. Signs carry meaning. Animals communicate information.

Mountain culture of the underworld is off limits. It is off limits to technology and the media. It is off limits to strangers. It is blanketed, secreted away. As a child I stumbled into the underworld and fell below into another dimension. Then I forgot the experience and trekked my way into adulthood. I forgot until, as an adult, the serpent reappeared in Scottsdale, Arizona, claiming that the underworld wanted me back. I could have ignored its invitation. There was no insistence. It simply seemed natural to accept.

With the serpent's invitation, I began living in parallel realities. Above and below. I maintained my family, job, and friends, while experiencing conscious visitations by creatures who seemed more suitable for Saturday morning cartoons. These creatures are inhabitants of what I call the underworld dimension. Other cultures and other researchers may use another term. I choose the term underworld because of my vivid childhood memory of coming up from and out of its invisible boundary.

Creatures of the underworld dimension are primarily **reptilian**. They are large, sometimes seven to eight foot standing reptiles. I can "feel" their dry scaly skin. Sometimes their skin reflects a glowing iridescent light. I sense their powerful and purposeful energy. I discriminate between them—male, female, familiar, stranger. They appear and hover just outside my conscious mind until I communicate. They seem to inhabit a world within our world. A dimension just outside our reality.

Other creatures from the underworld appear as serpents, standing snakes. They too are large beings. Like reptiles, these serpents communicate with me. Are they the Old Testament Garden of Eden variety of serpent? Perhaps. They seem capable of wisdom and healing. Accompanying the reptiles and serpents are gentle, wise, praying mantis type creatures. Tall, thin, angular, limbed creatures, they constantly move with a gentle motion. Their elbow joints open and close as they manifest. Huge dark eyes wrap their narrow heads. They feel shy, with a startling intellect, wisdom, and knowledge.

As my ability to communicate with these creatures increased, so did the frequency of our contact. A relationship ensued. A trust developed.

I understood that I was dealing with a dimension known to many of my ancestors. It was a dimension hidden and forgotten, or perhaps shunned and ignored for fear of persecution. The experience of my ancestors was probably no different than the Irish who talk of the fairies and leprechauns, who pop out of the ground to play with children in the garden and woodlands. Only I didn't see cute fairies in childhood, I saw seven and eight foot creatures. A "big" difference.

Fortunately, my underworld experience was authenticated by relationships I was forming in Arizona. A friend introduced me to an internationally eminent anomalous researcher, Dr. Ruth Hover. She became my mentor and friend. If there was a Native American, alternative history or UFO book, Dr. Ruth had read it and added it to her library. Active in researching anomalous phenomenon since the 1950s, she had ties to many of the post-war research institutes. To this day, she maintains an impressive global network of fellow researchers who trust her scientific mind, archival memory, and network of colleagues.

I joined Dr. Ruth's monthly "contact group." It was composed of professional people, parents, and young adults, united through their extraterrestrial contact experience. The group was the first place I found acceptance and calm acknowledgement of my experiences. Everyone was on the same frequency. None were afraid or panic stricken by their contact. It was a fact of their life.

Luckily I found Dr. Ruth's group before I found David Icke's books. In ufology there are individuals, like Icke, who vilify reptilian underworld energies. They link them to the Illuminati, to shape-shifters, to evil manipulators of wealth and the desire for a domineering world government. They link them to the cabal and the secret government. They cloak all purported reptilian experiences to conspiracy.

Eager for any reptilian information, I read David Icke's books. I respect his research and experiences. But, they are not mine. And yet, I agree with many of his conclusions. No doubt, as Icke maintains, reality is not what we deem it to be. My dimensional experiences validated that. No doubt the wealthy gather to network privately, set agendas, and make decisions. This seemed a probable political reality. No doubt, certain individuals shape shift to reveal another nature. Shamans make a habit of it when they astral travel. No doubt reptilian energy is ancient and difficult to comprehend. No doubt individuals in our government and military know of these underworld, reptilian energies and perhaps work with them. Icke demonized the reptilian underworld dimension and those who associated with and misused its energies. As I lived with these energies, critical judgments faded.

Reptilians are real. They dwell in another dimension. They can be communicated with and related to. They can be respected and trusted. They provide and maintain an active inter-dimensional portal. Re-entering this portal in adulthood, I experienced their reality with a mature perspective. Reptilian reality threads through human reality. It manifests in Bible stories, myths, legends, and art. Reptilian reality anchors human reality. Through them, earth secrets are revealed. Through them, earth structures are maintained and protected.

As I reacquainted with the underworld, I began to uncover ancient wisdom—sacred geometry, number, vibration, energy. My earth citizenship as a "crust dweller" expanded into deep levels of esoteric knowledge. Like a rabbit transfixed by a snake, I shifted into altered states of consciousness where the fabric of life had a different texture. Architecture and structure became a science of proportion and beauty. Viewing exquisite buildings triggered a deep sense of satisfaction, a familiar vibration. Agriculture and its seasons of sowing seeds, then nurturing plants to harvest expanded into the esoteric science of *crop circles*. Throughout the world, but primarily in Avebury, Stonehenge, and Silbury Hill, England, crop circles appear in late summer, just prior to harvest. They imprint the earth with geometric, mathematical symbols for the eager initiate to decipher using science and metaphysics. Every summer new messages appear on the surface of the earth.

Through the reptilian lens, art and myth focus. Story is reality. Whether it was ancient myths like Isis and Osiris, or Persephone in the underworld, or Jason and the Golden Fleece, each of these stories ring true as the reality of the underworld. Yes, humans journey through the portal of the underworld and return to tell of their adventure. All humans journey through the underworld, either conscious or unconscious. The choice is yours. Being human, you possess a cord to underworld environs. You can travel the cord—awake or asleep. Once the blindfold is removed, you have the ability to travel and encounter an inter-dimensional underworld community.

Eyes open, aware, you can choose to view the underworld as demonic, cruel, and controlling. There are many like Icke who share this view. If it were up to them, everyone would cut the cord and be free of the underworld. You would then reject the human reality of the underworld perceived as controlling and dangerous.

Or, eyes open, aware, you can choose to view the underworld as simply another dimension to explore and consciously inhabit. To do this, you need to suspend judgment and expectations. Then, you can learn to navigate its terrain, and in so doing, learn about yourself and earth dimensions. Eyes open, aware, the underworld becomes one among multiple dimensions. Reptilian reality becomes one of many dimensional realities inhabited with intelligent beings. Human, living on planet earth, you begin to see yourself as part of an inter-dimensional reality.

Bring on the underworld myths, they no longer frighten. Bring on the hideous monsters, they no longer lurk in the dark. Bring on the next visit, you know you will easily return, wiser and more mature. It is not a matter of conquering the underworld dimension. It is not a matter of denying the underworld dimension. It is not a matter of demonizing the underworld dimension. Instead, it is simply a matter of owning the part of your human nature that is corded to its reality. In so doing, ancient knowledge, once secret and forbidden, opens to reveal its simplicity and truth.

Ancient underworld knowledge includes innate human abilities to sense earth vibrations, to find your way on the earth using psychic sense. Celtic tradition tells of blindfolding children, leaving them like Hansel and Gretel in the woods. Parents trusted the child's psychic earth-centered abilities to find their way home. Have you ever traveled and found your way without compass or stars? That ability may be linked to your innate underworld abilities.

As global warming intensifies and earth changes move over populations like a tidal wave, underworld wisdom leads the way to protection and safety. Like reptiles, humans may need to burrow to survive. Underworld energies protect and maintain the structure of planet earth. Underworld wisdom is ancient and timely. Have you ever sensed an impending earthquake or storm? That ability may be linked to your innate underworld abilities. Intuitively, you know when it is time to take cover.

Your relation to the underworld is simple and yet complex. At one point I discovered that beings in the underworld dimension, like humans, were open to realigning relationships. After years of communication with reptilians and other underworld beings and energies, I felt it was time to move on. I needed to reorder the relationship. I needed to put some detachment and distance between us. I wanted to respect our lines of communication, yet I needed to detach from their energies. And so, I simply requested that we reconfigure our relationship. We dialogued for several days and then we realigned. I have a vivid memory of declaring to them that the time of my initiation and education was over. Our intense time, almost like a courtship, had ended. I wanted to communicate and relate to them on different terms. We negotiated, and then agreed.

Reptilians still appear and communicate. I travel to the underworld, though less frequently. I honor our relationship and the energy we share. They are intimately connected to our earth dimension. I know that somehow—through DNA or bloodline or frequency—I am connected to them. That may never change. What did change was my naïve perspective of who I am and how I shape my reality. I shape my reality through respect and knowledge, not through fear. I acknowledge myself as an inter-dimensional being—not a flatlander of three dimensions. I thank reptilians for this orientation and wisdom.

Reptilian Legacy to the Stars

Confusing questions rise when links appear between dimensions. Connectedness is fraught with questions. How does the reptilian underworld correlate with extraterrestrials? If I cord to the underworld do I also cord to the stars and inter-galactic dimensions? Yes, underworld, cosmic and earth dimensions are inter-related, interconnected. Your human legacy is the underworld and the stars. Many extraterrestrial contactees report witnessing alien cosmic grey type beings working alongside underworld reptilian beings. For example, Jim Sparks, an abductee interviewed by journalist, Linda Moulton Howe in her book *Glimpses of Other Realities, Vol II* reported an underworld visitation with extraterrestrial components.

While living in North Carolina and working in real estate development, Jim had a series of encounters. Awakened in the middle of the night by a low pitched whirling sound, he felt himself pulled down. Then he became aware of being transported through the wall and on to a craft. In the craft, he identified small alien **grays** as workers, tall aliens as supervisors, and tall reptoids with scaly reptile skin as overseers. On board the craft, during a series of encounters, Jim learned to decipher alien symbols and language. He reported learning to read from right to left, bottom to top, seeing three dimensional letters and symbols. He claims he could feel and see the words.

Similar to Jim Sparks' contact experience, our human origins are linked to underworld and cosmic dimensions that seem to co-exist with our earth life of three dimensions plus time. And yet, many in the scientific research community scoff at alternative researchers eager to explore cosmic and underworld dimensions.

Researchers studying our possible extraterrestrial origins are currently on a divergent research tangent, largely ignored by the scientific community. Few mainline researchers embrace the possibility of human connection and legacy to dimensional realities. Most extraterrestrial, underworld research remains independent. Yet, despite the exclusion, a growing number of independent researchers are opening the door to important information. These independent researchers are trained academic scholars who hold themselves to high research standards, regardless of the present separation from their academic community. Due to their research commitment and public communication, information on our possible extraterrestrial origins is becoming widely available.

The godfather of extraterrestrial origins research is Zacharia Sitchin, a Biblical scholar knowledgeable in modern and ancient Hebrew, Old Testament, Semitic, and European languages. Sitchin researched ancient Sumerian documents for 30 years prior to the publication of *The Twelfth Planet* in 1976.

According to Sitchin, Sumer, which was biblical Shin'ar, was situated on the plain between the Tigris and Euphrates, site of current-day Iraq. This ancient civilization held knowledge of the full solar system with all outer planets, including Uranus, discovered in 1781, Neptune, discovered in 1846, and Pluto, discovered in 1930. The Sumerian story of the planet Earth's creation is that when Planet **Nibiru**, ("Planet of the Crossing" or "Planet X") entered our solar system, one of its moons collided with planet Tiamat, breaking it in two. One segment exploded into an asteroid belt and one segment emerged as planet Earth.

Planet Nibiru, according to the Sumerians and Sitchin, is on a large elliptical orbit that brings it into our solar system between Mars and Jupiter every 3,600 years. Its arrival is announced with comet-like tail ancients called the "seed of life."

Sitchin's research also uncovered evidence of our human origins linked to the Annunaki, a race whose home planet was Nibiru. This same Annunaki race is linked to underworld reptilians and controlling Illuminati factions of conspiracy theory. According to Sitchin, the extraterrestrial, and later Earth dwelling and underworld **Annunaki** beings created humans by a carefully conceived union of their DNA with the most advanced human life form on earth at the time. According to Sitchin, Sumerian records cite the creation of advanced humans by the Annunaki for the purpose of mining gold and working as slaves. (No wonder the veins of West Virgina hold their secrets.)

Despite the fact that immortality was not granted this hybrid human, these hybrid humans caused no end of grief for the Annunaki. The Sumerian documents relate a decision by an angered Enlil, one of the Annunaki leaders, to cause a global catastrophic flood and weather upheavals to wipe the troublesome hybrid human off the face of the earth. The *Epic of Gilgamesh* tells the story of another Annunaki, Enki, who was dedicated to protecting humans, against his angry elder brother's wishes. Enki instructed select humans to build a vessel to survive the floods. Of course, this flood story is retold in many versions throughout the world. The best known to the Western world is the Old

Testament Noah story. This seems an obvious retelling of the *Epic of Gilgamesh.*

A primary religious resource for mainstream Sunday sermons and biblical teaching, *The Interpreter's Bible*, briefly references the Sumerian and Babylonians as the basis of the Old Testament. According to Fretheim, a contributor in the Genesis volume, "Israel drew on a widespread fund of images and ideas to shape into a creation story." He cites the similarity of the Old Testament creation story with Babylonian *Enuma Elis*, the *Epic of Atrahasis,* and the Egyptian creation account that emphasized "the word." Then he cites dissimilarities between the Old Testament and the Sumerian Babylonian creation. According to Fretheim, the Old Testament account differs distinctly from the Sumerian Babylonian. The Old Testament account lacks: a) theogony (listing of Gods), b) conflict among the Gods, and c) prevailing monotheism. Similarities between the Old Testament and Babylonia creation include: a) images of God as a potter, working with existing materials, b) God fighting with and achieving victory over chaotic forces.

Eventually, research of ancient sources, aided by technology advances, will weave the slender threads separating creation stories. A holistic, integrated retelling of creation allows humans a clearer understanding of who we are, and where we came from, in order to move forward.

Will Hart in *The Genesis Race: Our Extraterrestrial DNA and the True Origins of the Species* researches the creation stories of the Old Testament, uncovering a possible extraterrestrial presence. According to Hart, the two creation stories, Genesis 1 and 2 present divergent creation stories. Genesis 1 outlines the familiar seven days of creation and Genesis 2 outlines the creation of man from dust and the Garden of Eden. Citing both creation stories, Hart points to the confusion between Yahweh, one God, creating man in his own image and **Elohim**, or the plural "Let us make man in **our** image" (*The New Oxford Annotated*

Bible, Gen.1.26). Whether the God of creation is singular or plural, Genesis reflects an almost human nature on to our creator. Genesis 3.8 refers to the "sound of the Lord walking in the Garden." Genesis 3.9 refers to the Lord calling to man "Where are you?" The Lord then makes a garment for Adam and Eve. Genesis 6.2 tells what happened when the "sons of God saw the daughters of man." These scriptures are often used to refer to the race of giants or the **Nephilim** who occupied Earth.

Finally Hart refers to the human nature of angelic appearances in the Old Testament as another indication of extraterrestrial origins. In Genesis 19, Lot is sitting at the gates of Sodom as the Angels approach. They go to Lot's house where they eat and speak. Hart asserts that Old Testament Angels and God(s) of creation who walk and talk may be extraterrestrial beings. Talking, walking, sewing, reproducing all indicate that the God(s) of the Old Testament had human-like qualities and abilities. Hart indicates that the ancient storytellers were describing our extraterrestrial ancestors who also may have been instrumental in our creation.

The **Dead Sea Scrolls** and **Nag Hammadi**, additional source documents of the Old Testament, also provide information on our possible extraterrestrial origins. The Dead Sea Scrolls contain fragments of the **books of Enoch** in Aramaic. Enoch was known as the first among the "children of men" born on the Earth with knowledge of writing, science, and wisdom from the Angels. According to Andrew Collins in his book, *From the Ashes of Angels,* Watchers are a specific divine race of Angels, "meaning those who watch or those who are awake." These Watchers are Angels sent from the Lord. They come down to Earth to instruct humans to bring about justice and equality. Enoch travels to heaven to meet with the Angels to testify about the interbreeding among Watchers and humans. Punishment was determined to come by flooding the Earth.

The creation story of the Nag Hammadi describes the bodies of Adam and Eve as overlaid with horny skin that was bright as daylight, like a luminescent garment, such that they didn't need clothing. The description of Adam and Eve's skin sounds reptilian. In an article in *Fate Magazine*, Joe Lewels describes the Garden of Eden encounter of these reptilian beings. As Adam and Eve ate from the tree of knowledge, "She took some of its fruit and ate, and she gave to her husband also…then their minds opened. For when they ate, the light of knowledge shone for them. When they saw their makers, they loathed them since they were beastly forms. They understood very much."

These biblical source documents creation stories reference a possible extraterrestrial superhuman reptilian race involved in human creation. Contemporary scientists concur. Neurologists cite the vestiges of human reptilian heritage in the core of the human brain. The R-complex, or **reptilian complex** is responsible for aggressive behavior, territoriality, ritual, and social hierarchies. The middle brain, or limbic system, represents the human mammalian heritage. This part of the brain is responsible for feelings of love, hate, compassion, and sentimentality. The outer layer of the brain or the neo-cortex is responsible for reasoning, deliberation, and the place where we determine the difference between good and evil.

As ancient biblical source documents are examined using technology and as lost books become accessible, our extraterrestrial lineage may become more apparent and less threatening. Our concept of God(s) may need to readjust and broaden as the reality of our divine maker emerges. Those familiar with research concerning our extraterrestrial origins are forging new territory, characterizing certain behaviors and attributes as "star seed." As details about our creators emerge, human extraterrestrial-like abilities become commonplace. Like our creators, we see ourselves moving naturally among dimensions as telepathic, psychic, vibration beings that can teleport and time travel.

With the Underworld work…there is a property of human consciousness—
Something that happens in our awareness. We tend to project it onto the past, but it's really not the past or the future, but some kind of timeless present we step through.
R.J. Stewart

Chapter 7
Underworld Stairway to the Stars

The underworld was a confusing, strange, alluring dimension. As a child, I was certain of its reality, and yet nothing in my daily life related to its existence. No one discussed its beings. Adults seemed unaware of its existence. Other children did not share stories of their visits. I was alone with my visions and visitations.

Solitary underworld visits did not bother me; it was natural to be underneath the ground, alone. I had no idea why I was there or what I was supposed to be doing. It never occurred to me to define underworld reality through the lens of my daily earth life. It was simply a place I visited.

Later in childhood, when I could read, I received a scattering of clues, breadcrumbs forming a fragmentary conception of the underworld. Growing up in a minister's home, I was saturated with Bible stories and golden picture book images of Hebrew stories. My parents gave my brother and me a book series that included a book called *All about Archeology.* Intuitively I knew that the underworld related to the images in that book from archeological digs in Sumeria, Mesopotamia, and Egypt. Their vivid drawings pulled me into their world.

As I slid down turquoise, royal blue, purple, red, and gold shafts of images into the underworld, I became aware of another reality—one I would much later decipher. I was keenly aware that my soul was in the underground and that I needed to reunite. I clung to the images in the *All About Archeology* book. As a child I believed that if I could dig deep enough I would reunite with my soul. All would be well.

And so the expedition began. Religion was the first door I opened. In college and graduate school, I studied philosophy, religion, theology, myth, and ritual. I practiced my professional ministerial role and sifted through rituals and rites for clues. I became a university chaplain, knowing that I belonged on the fringe. As an ecumenical chaplain, I was employed by nine protestant denominations. Furthermore, I teamed with the Roman Catholic chaplains, and since the campus had no Hillel or Muslim leadership, I developed programming for Jewish and Islamic students. I learned the myth, rituals, and beliefs of many religions. Yet, the secrets of the underworld remained illusive.

Moving to Arizona I related to Native American spirituality and their traditions of communicating with Star Visitors. Phoenix was the perfect home for the next phase of my expedition. I studied extraterrestrials and UFOs, later to be mesmerized by Jaime Maussan's craft consciousness. Craft sightings filled the Phoenix skies. March 13, 1997 a silent, perhaps mile-long V-shaped craft traveled through a main traffic corridor of Arizona. Dr. Lynne Kitei, a Paradise Valley physician, witnessed and photographed similar lights in 1995 and then again during the Phoenix Lights mass sighting in 1997. Her independent research culminated in the award-winning documentary *The **Phoenix Lights***. Worldwide sightings of V-shaped craft continue today.

While I did not witness the lights, since I was teaching Extraterrestrial Reality at Scottsdale Community College, Dr. Kitei graciously included me in her documentary. Through the experiencers group led by Dr.

Ruth Hover and a growing collection of Phoenix researchers I joined a vital, active ufology community.

Despite my dedication to the scientific, political, historical, and psychological aspects of ufology and extraterrestrial contact, the pull of the underworld remained. There was an underworld—extraterrestrial connection. With my ufology colleagues excited about sightings, contact experiences, or the latest government disclosure, again and again I returned to the underworld. It was counter-intuitive. Ufologists were above; I was below. Yet, I possessed an intuitive certainty that the path through the underworld led to the stars. Crazy, but it felt right.

Then the doors of ancient Egypt opened. Egyptian religion or more accurately, Egyptian lifestyle referenced a necessary path through the underworld into the stars. Scholars like Jeremy Naydler, who wrote *Temple of the Cosmos*, provide a detailed explanation of the Egyptian underworld journey.

As you cross the threshold of Egyptian scholarship, you may enter a familiar realm. Viewing the Underworld through Egyptian lens affirmed my childhood experiences. It deepened my understanding of consciousness, UFO's, extraterrestrials, and multiple dimensions of reality. To understand who we are, to whom we are tied and where we are headed—Egyptian wisdom is essential.

According to Naydler, like religion and spirituality today, the Egyptians followed two distinct paths through the underworld to the stars, depending on one's orientation. One path was communal and religious. Initiates traveled through the underworld in a closely guarded group. There was little or no independent thought or movement. Religious dogma and doctrines lighted their way. Most of the knowledge of the stars was promised after death. As a group they moved through the underworld into the stars, reaching their destination after death.

Another group, primarily royalty and spiritually oriented, was permitted to journey the underworld alone, consciously receiving the illumination of the stars during their earthly life. Completing the journey, they became the middle point, the human fulcrum between the living and the dead, between the underworld and the stars.

Both the individual and the group moved through similar levels of initiation. The first level involved meeting with *Ka,* their vital life force residing in the unconscious. Like Protestant Lutheran theology, the Egyptian group initiates believed their *Ka* was a gift from an outside divine source. Their concept was similar to Martin Luther's theology that human salvation was dependent on the gift of grace through faith, which we receive through Jesus Christ. This Lutheran theological doctrine provided communal strength for a religious journey. Egyptian group initiates also believed that in death they go to join their *Ka* group. Christian Gospels reflected the communal Egyptian message as Jesus spoke to his disciples of eternal life, promising to go to prepare a place for them (as a group). Like their Egyptian forbearers, Christian group initiatives gain solace and strength through the Gospel assurances of a group destination to heaven or eternal life.

In contrast, the Egyptian royalty had conscious access to the *Ka* and were able to assimilate this life force during their earthly life. Each independently accessed their *Ka.* (Perhaps termed the *Ka* within.) This *Ka* was a spiritual double with a physical, flesh body, often portrayed as a twin. As such, royalty could consciously unite with their *Ka,* complete underworld initiations, and emerge into the stars during this earthly life. Though not stated, royalty's access to the stars might have the potential for repeated journeys. Once you learn the path, the way is open.

One of the Egyptian underworld initiations involved the *Ba,* or the soul. The soul was a spiritual force that could be accessed in altered, psychic states. Was *Ba* the soul of my childhood buried in the underworld? If so, my experience during this life led me to it. *Ba* is accessed in out-of-body states. The physical body lies like a corpse and the *Ba* is released to move to heaven.

One vivid experience of the *Ba* initiation was becoming conscious of floating above one's body. While most religions don't encourage astral travel or out-of-body experiences, they are quite common. (Despite the Egyptian belief they are only for royal bloodlines.) Vivid recollection of floating out of and above our bodies happens during near death experiences as well as during common everyday life. Over lunch, a young mother once told how her son nudged her during a church service to say that he had been floating on the ceiling looking down at his body. Despite being schussed for talking during church, he had successfully launched out with his *Ba*. He popped out of his physical body, looked around, and then traveled back. As metaphysics teaches, we are connected by an umbilical like cord, such that our *Ba* never completely separates from our physical body. I sometimes envision it like party toys—big inflated balls with elastic bands that attach to the wrist. Children play with the inflated ball as it bounces back and forth to and from their body on the elastic band. Our *Ba,* or soul, likes to travel, usually in dreamtime, but when we are relaxed, playful, or even bored it will separate from our physical body, have a look around, and then return home.

Another level of underworld initiation involved the Egyptian *Akh*, which is the power of self-regeneration or rebirth. This rebirth or remembering occurs when the initiate is reunited with the stars or *Ra*. For the communal group, reconnection with the stars takes place after death, when the initiate becomes a spiritual body, all limbs intact. This marks the final liberation from the underworld into the stars. For royalty, the journey to the stars is a conscious, lifetime experience.

So what is this Egyptian underworld? The underworld is the time between day and night or twilight. Anyone who has timed the setting sun sliding into the horizon, especially an ocean horizon, knows the fleeting time of twilight. The underworld can be accessed consciously during life and after death. It is a dimension. It has reality. It can be accessed, traveled, and experienced. Egyptians characterized it as a place of learning through trial and error, moving across and through boundaries. Journeys through the underworld flavor and enhance our earth-life. Underworld journeys can consume you, frighten you, or you can relax in the knowledge that it is a reality that belongs to all humans. You can ignore it, push it deep into our unconscious, or you can enter and enjoy. I chose to enter and enjoy.

Sure, like a game, the underworld involves luck, trial and error, patience and perseverance. You believe you are all knowing and moving into the winner's circle when up from behind comes another trial and you are back to square one. In the underworld, you may experience being upside down, in a hall of mirrors where the familiar is strange. You may hear voices that threaten or comfort. You may be lost in total darkness. Feelings vacillate from total loss and abandonment to embarking on a voyage of serenity and ease sailing through uncharted waters. You may feel juiced and euphoric one minute and suffocating in an alien airless environment the next. As one experience follows the next, negative confusing energy can surround the initiate. The trick is not to explode, eliminate, or evaporate the negative energy. Instead, the patient traveler turns the negative energy upon itself, thereby transforming and owning it. Each demon owned by the initiate is named, brought into conscious awareness, and befriended.

The underworld is not a computer game that a programmer filled with action. No two people play the same game. The underworld is an individualized, customized journey with programming sourced in eternity. As such, it just is. Play the game, or don't.

Know that if you choose to play and enter the underworld the reward is great. You move down and then out into the cosmos. But you cannot "pass go"—into the cosmos—until you master the underworld. The final levels of mastery are where you learn to awaken and rebirth—all on your own. You become like an infant who learns to self-soothe and falls asleep without the rocking motion of a parent. The initiate leaves the underworld capable of cracking their own shell and awakening to a new cosmic perspective. This cosmic perspective involves inner equilibrium, a balancing of opposites, through transformation of negative opposing forces confronted in the underworld. All underworld demons become gods. You reach a state where there are no gods or demons, only individual divine cosmic consciousness. There is no need to wait until death to be united with God or a group consciousness. You are complete within and without.

Once you become a master, in the end, you possess cosmic consciousness. Yet, the underworld remains and can always be reentered. While journeying through the underworld, you can mine the core of your being. You can finally choose the point of re-membering where your soul, spirit, and body are one. Out of the underworld, you can navigate the heavens and swim in the waters of cosmic consciousness, drawn into the light of source. Home.

Obelisk Exercise

Benefits of Exercise:

- Experiencing being simultaneously rooted and inter-dimensional
- Becoming a human antenna

Is this underworld discussion all gibberish? If so, try this exercise. It is ancient. It is what anchors Paris, Washington, Rome, and Egypt.

Imagine your body becoming an obelisk. Imagine your body becoming the Washington Monument, simultaneously soaring toward the cosmos and then reflected in the waters of the reflecting pool. Imagine yourself as a oneness of three dimensions underworld, earth, and cosmos.

Stand with your feet grounded, about a shoulder-width apart. Breathe deeply then exhale, conscious of your brain and body filling with air. As your body fills with oxygen, you begin to feel somewhat lightheaded. Now, regulate and calm your breathing.

Imagine a place deep in the earth. A place where your core being resides. Imagine an earthen, clay figure of you emerging from this core. As your image grows, imagine a cord attached to the top of the head of the figure that extends up into the left sole of your foot. This cord transmits light from your core self of the underworld into your physical body. Allow the light to move through your body, eventually coming out the top of your head and up into a shaft of cosmic light. This cosmic light travels to your eternal source. It is your path. It belongs to no one but you. It is your connection to your source.

Connect to your cosmic, star source, and then bring the light back down into your body entering your head and traveling down the right side of your body, back into the core earth figure. You are obelisk. Heaven, earth, and underworld. You become a conscious circuit moving wisdom, information, love, and pure energy. That is you, at one with yourself.

Isn't it astonishing that all these secrets have been preserved for so many years just so we could discover them!
Orville Wright

Chapter 8
Disappearing Daytonians

The skies above Phoenix are alive. Military, commercial, private, and experimental aircraft crisscross the clear sky. It is a perfect environment for flight. It is an environment very different from Dayton, Ohio, where I located after leaving West Virginia. Unlike Phoenix, Dayton is dense with cloud cover, forest, and farmland and yet it birthed modern flight. My husband and I renovated an historical home near the bicycle shop where the Wright brothers tinkered until they successfully applied the dynamics of flight. Later, we moved and raised our children down the street from the Wright brothers' landmark home. A portrait of their sister, Catherine Wright, greeted us when we went to the library for story time.

Like the Wright brothers, I inherited deep religious roots from my father and a strong intelligent mother. The Wright brother's father, Milton, was a Bishop in the United Brethren Church, so they developed an independent spirit and a strong, conservative work ethic. Germanic, dogged determination through methodical process characterized United Brethrens. Dogged determination coupled with a love for the religious quest, especially when it involved analysis and questioning. The Wright Brothers' mother, Susan Koerner Wright, secured their intellectual foundation. She schooled them in math and science. A brilliant mother seems essential for an innovative child's success.

While people in West Virginia vanished underground, people in Dayton disappeared into their garages. The Engineers Club was the gathering place for men who tinkered weekends in their garages and during the workday in labs and factories. Intrigued by possibilities not yet known, puzzles not yet solved, they created the next generation of machines. The Wright Brothers created flying machines and left a lineage for others to pursue experimental aircraft. Other Dayton inventors created the stepladder, auto starter, electrical stimulation for ambulatory movement of paralyzed persons, the flip-top-can, and the mood ring. Others extended our venture into space with inventions like the parachute, propellers, and spacecraft generators. Myths and legends flourished around these Dayton inventors. Caught by the inspiration of making something better or new, they quietly disappeared into their garages to create.

Armies of subsidiary manufacturers and professionals gathered to support Dayton inventors. Patent attorneys, tool and dye shops, steel companies, machinists, welders, electricians, and computer technicians flanked the inventors.

Many inventors were German—precise, introverted, and intelligent. Perfectionism marked the intricate carpentry of porches and architectural detail of their homes. Perfection calculated minute machining calibrations before computer programs. Their hands felt the imperfection; their eyes caught a flaw before CNC. It was commonplace for businesses to birth down some back alley, in a garage workshop, only to merge into a multi-national corporation. Dayton soil was fertile for invention.

Like many in Dayton, my family carried familiar German ancestry. My father was a Fisher. In Dayton he served a church that held German-speaking services. Coming from the Brethren heritage, he had been raised in Germanic communities and felt at ease with this new congregation. They welcomed our family as we acquainted ourselves with their strict, private lifestyles and mechanical brilliance.

Completing my seminary graduate education I was ordained in the United Methodist denomination. As an ecumenical chaplain, for many years I worked at Wright State University adjacent to Wright Patterson Air Force Base, reported home of the famed **Roswell** artifacts. Hanger 18 at Wright Patterson was the legendary storage site of the Roswell craft.

Whether the artifacts of Roswell ever resided at Wright Field, the UFO phenomenon began in earnest with that crash. The 1947 Roswell incident spawned a plethora of stories. How did technology advance so exponentially, after WWII? In ufology, two theories have emerged. Colonel Corso, in his book, *The Day After Roswell,* describes how the Army parceled out artifacts from alien crash debris to other branches of the military and corporations for research and development. Michael Salla, in his book, *Exopolitics: Political Implications of the Extraterrestrial Presence,* theorizes that a series of formal treaties were drawn up between our government and aliens that may have allowed for direct transmission of extraterrestrial technology.

Regardless of the sources, alien treaties and or crash retrievals such as Roswell, our post-war culture moved through a period of rapid technical advancement—lasers, fiber optics, integrated circuitry, night vision, zero-point energy, invisible armor, and **artificial intelligence**. Even virtual reality goggles worn by today's gamers may have been developed from the mind-craft interface technology discovered on the retrieved craft at Roswell. In some strange way, Colonel Corso and others believed that the craft and the crew were one. Craft instrumentation seemed one with the mind of the crew. Craft consciousness.

Colonel Corso, believed that the aliens found at the crash site were hybrids. He hypothesized that alien hybrids were specifically created to fly inter-dimensionally without sustaining physical or mental trauma. Perhaps they were hybrids. Perhaps they are similar to what humans will be in the future. Human bodies and minds accelerate as we invent and use new technologies. The ability to cope with dramatic climate change, live in space stations outside our familiar atmosphere, and time travel inter-dimensionally require human cells, organs, and minds to transform. Even now, our transformation is accelerating rapidly and radically. Are we an endangered species? Like the gorilla, condor, red wolf, or tiger? Or are our bodies capable of cellular transformation? Might humans someday look like the grays portrayed in movies like *Communion*? Might humans evolve into humanoids that look like us but are semi-robotic? Might some of us move underground and develop reptilian characteristics? One certainty remains—humans are changing. And the crash retrieval at Roswell accelerated the change.

Details of the storage and dispersal of the Roswell artifacts remain a mystery. However, if they were shipped to Wright Field in Dayton, they fell on fertile ground, to be tended by a unique culture of inventors. I believe more than one inventor, working in his garage, was given the opportunity to glimpse future possibilities from the Roswell crash. I believe more than one Dayton inventor glimpsed the artifacts and caught the inextinguishable inspiration to doggedly, perfectly, and practically apply inherent scientific principles of the artifact, creating radical inventions we use today.

If it really happened, we may never know. But, I'll bet it did. Historically, the government and military, coming out of WWII were overwhelmed by alien sightings and crash retrievals, Roswell in particular. The Truman and then Eisenhower administrations made crucial decisions to fold the UFO, alien phenomenon into a blanket of secrecy. The secrecy decision was understandable. They did not know whom or what they were dealing with. Furthermore, they were handling the rise of international powers—Soviet Union, Korea, China—not to mention their need to quickly integrate German rocket science and reported craft experimentation into our military technology.

Operation Paperclip, officially established in 1945, began the undercover transfer of German scientists into American research and industry. It solved the issue of transferring advanced German technology into the American military industrial complex. Figures vary regarding the numbers of German scientists who relocated to the US. There seems to have been well over 500. Were German scientists relocated to Dayton and Wright Patterson? No doubt. There was a community of peers— engineers, scientists, inventors—ready to receive them. As German scientists arrived they may have moved into familiar gingerbread homes designed by local craftsmen from their homeland. They may have quietly filled neighborhoods of German speaking churches, and local restaurants serving wurst and beer. Their comfort equation was complete. They made a silent, easy assimilation into the American military, industrial, cultural complex.

Silently, Paperclip communities spread to designated sites across America. The White Sands, New Mexico group lived in an isolated desert military installation. Researching hermits, hopefully they relished the dry, dusty desert. Many Europeans love the fantasy of the West. Wherever they migrated, these scientists silently integrated—their private lives into local communities and their intellectual genius into the American military complex.

Note: In their book, *Exempt from Disclosure,* Robert Collins and Richard Doty provide an in-depth discussion of Hanger 18 and the role of Wright Patterson Air Force Base in craft retrieval.

Alien artifacts, treaties, craft retrievals, Project Paperclip—researchers continue to collect whistleblower testimony and historical documents that verify the seeding of alien knowledge into our post-WWII military-industrial culture. Scholars like Michael Salla risk their academic careers to investigate possible face-to-face alien-government meetings and agreements. As documents and eyewitness accounts accumulate, not only does the reality of alien face-to-face meetings seem feasible, but also possible crucial decisions and alliances emerge.

Michael Salla was dismissed from American University after a 2004 *Washington Post* article disclosed his research regarding Eisenhower's alleged 1954 meeting with extraterrestrials at Edward's Air Force Base.

In his article, *Eisenhower's 1954 Meeting with Extraterrestrials,* Salla contends that the night of February 20 to 21, 1954, during a vacation in Palm Springs, California, Eisenhower disappeared. The next morning he reappeared at a press conference and explained his disappearance as a dental emergency. According to a California metaphysical leader, Gerald Light, Eisenhower did not go to the dentist, but joined Franklin Allen of Hearst Papers, Edwin Nourse of Brookings Institute, and Bishop MacIntyre of the Los Angeles Catholic Church in an arranged meeting with extraterrestrials. Light termed the extraterrestrials "Etherians" and noted the confusion, chaos, and his dramatic shift in beliefs as the aliens approached in their craft.

Who were these alleged aliens? According to Salla, William Cooper, of the Naval Intelligence briefing team, claimed there were two meetings with grays from the Orion star system. A controversial source in UFO circles, Cooper described them as the large-nosed, **tall gray** alien race. Michael Wolfe, another government insider in extraterrestrial affairs, claimed the meeting was with grays from Zeta Reticulum.

Cooper alleges that over the span of two meetings, a treaty was signed between our government and the grays. Salla cites researcher

Phil Schneider who termed it the "1954 Grenada Treaty." It granted the grays permission for animal testing (primarily cows) and limited human implants in exchange for technology.

But the treaty takes on a deeper meaning. According to Salla, Cooper alleges that prior to the meeting with the grays, a human-looking race met with government officials and offered expertise in spiritual development, under the condition that we would dismantle and destroy nuclear weapons. There was no offer of technology. According to Cooper, our government did not enter into this alliance due to humanoids' reluctance to exchange technological information and the condition requiring the dismantling of nuclear weaponry.

The investigative jury is still out as to the race(s) present, specific details of the alliances, and whether meetings occurred. Alien information may have infiltrated our culture through numerous conduits—face-to-face meetings, alien artifacts, retrieved crafts, and individual contact—accelerating both our technological and our spiritual evolvement. Certainly a post WWII overview of human advancement presents significant technological and spiritual leaps. Technological advances may reflect treaties and ongoing contact with tall grays. Meditation and mind control via focused intentionality, spiritual healing, energy medicine and the Peace Movement may reflect the results of ongoing contact with humanoid races.

Silent Post-War Heritage of Mind Control

Mind control—mental manipulation of the behavior of another—is often decried as cultish, demonic or illegal. Jonestown, Waco, satanic rituals, and pedophilia are sternly prosecuted. Yet, mind control is tightly woven into the fabric of everyday human interaction that we take for granted. For example, my attitudes, behaviors, and discipline tactics used to raise my children had a socially acceptable level of mind control. I was parent; they were child. We live in communities (religious, social, civic, and political) that exert control over behavior and beliefs. A smidgen of mind control is necessary in civilized society. But where do we draw the line between manipulative mind control and healthy discipline?

When I began my professional study of hypnosis, I realized that vast arenas of society deliberately misuse mind control. The media's use of mind control techniques to sell products or subliminally promote a message is well known. Ceaseless televised chatter suddenly did not seem so harmless to me. Teenagers and young adults continuously wired to iPods jolted me into an awareness of how easily we can slip into allowing another's agenda to invade our consciousness. Music and lyrics have mind power. Teenagers and young adults, of a tender, susceptible age, who love music, can be easily manipulated.

Then I discovered that religion, though well accepted by society, exhibited blatant use of hypnotic, mind control tactics. Of course these tactics were used to "connect" us to Jesus Christ, Buddha, or God. Chanting stimulates enlightenment, yet coercive individuals and groups can use these same tactics. Repetitive chanting, swaying, hymns, altered states of prayer and praise, terror, fear of punishment, singsong memorization of scripture—all of these are hypnotic. Fear of death is a powerful hypnosis. Punishment in hell is a powerful hypnosis. The few times I dared mention this aspect to religious colleagues, they vehemently disagreed. What they were doing was different, they argued. But, was it?

Even now, I am hypersensitive to repetitive chanting. When I am in the car with my friend, I ask her not to play her chanting CD's. They send chills through my mind. Buddhist, Catholic, Methodist, Muslim—religious leaders seem patently unaware of the hypnotic, mind control aspects of their traditions. Why? On some level, are they trained to believe that others need to be "tricked" into "believing?" What is so off-limits about a discussion of hypnotic mind control? Especially when it is so pervasive.

Society's mind control traditions are woven tightly into the fabric of our everyday, common life. The practices and methods are ancient. Current religious, political, and educational structures are built on an ignorance of the historical foundations of mind control tactics. Ancient Egyptian, Mayan, Indian, Chinese, African cultures flagrantly used trance tactics and rewarded those leaders who excelled at group mind control. Some things never change.

For a time, my knowledge of pervasive societal mind control tactics angered me. I felt personally affronted, persecuted. Then I began to acknowledge that mind control was simply a human activity. Trance results had varying degrees and durations of effectiveness. Certainly, religious practice of corralling young and tending them with a mindset well into adulthood was effective, albeit stifling to the individual. In a "civilized society" good religion makes good politics, makes good citizens. On a social scale, this cannot be disputed.

All mind control possesses a degree of manipulation, however slight. So, I determined to become conscious of not only my usage of these tactics, but also the myriad of ways they were employed on me. An eye-opening decision. As my awareness grew concerning my personal use of mind control, my anger against religion, politics, and society lessened. Are not we all victor and victim? Mind control is a human state of affairs. Am I glad I was angry at the extensive use and misuse of mind control? You bet. It allowed me to own my personal use of potentially manipulative mind tactics. Now I can consciously choose to participate...or not.

Project Paperclip, the relocation of German scientists into America, also included psychiatrists and psychologists who performed some of the most heinous mind control experiments in Nazi prison camps. And yes, these scientists and physicians quietly transferred their skill sets into American military and research facilities and communities. It is nauseating, frightening, and traumatic to read the post-war, Paperclip history of German-based mind control research in this country and Canada. Yet, it needs to be read. Like the history of lynching in the South or beheading in Muslim countries, or young female surgery in Africa—it all needs to be faced. Conscious awareness breathes release, light, and life into secret, silent corners of human history. I feel drawn to reveal this to you.

One of the most familiar post-war mind control personalities was Joseph Mengele, "angel of death." His morbid "medical" tactics on concentration camp inmates included surgery without anesthetic and experimenting with gradual freezing or suffocating. He allegedly transferred his trauma-based research from Berlin's Medical Institute to the United States via Paperclip, continuing his work in China Lake, California.

In 1953, another personality emerged. American chemist, Sidney Gottlieb, chief of the CIA's Technical Services Division, was appointed to head a government research and development program that used chemical and biological substances to affect human behavior. In, particular he experimented with LSD and other psychoactive drugs. The monikers attached to the program included Bluebird, Artichoke, and MKULTRA. Under Gottleib's leadership, teams of scientists researched and experimented with microwaves, drugs, and electromagnetics. There is scant public research available, but Nick Begich, M.D., in his book, *Controlling the Human Mind: The Technologies of Political Control or Tools for Peak Performance,* has compiled a thorough assessment of the positive and negative ramifications of mind control.

Canada participated with the United States in a mind control project headed by Dr. Ewen Cameron that honed brainwashing techniques. He is reported to have placed mentally ill patients in drug-induced comas for months while playing repetitive tapes. Cameron experimented in the 50s and 60s at the Allan Memorial Institute in Montreal, Canada. The documentary, *The Sleep Room*, based on Anne Collins' book, *In the Sleep Room: the Story of CIA Brainwashing Experiments in Canada*, detailed Cameron's excessive use of electroshock therapy and hallucinogenic drugs to control behavior and memory. Cameron, while heading this controversial research program, garnered professional acclaim as chair of the World Psychiatric Association and president of both the American and Canadian Psychiatric Associations. Is it any wonder that current psychiatric practices merged seamlessly with the pharmaceutical industry?

It is undeniable that the legacy of military funded mind control research also spawned positive improvements in human health. Alternative healers use electromagnetic pulses to control mental and physical abilities. Primordial sound with crystal bowls and Buddhist chanting assist in calming and centering the mind. Further, it assists with transforming the mind to an enlightened state. Mainstream physicians use bio-feedback for pain management. Scientific research on light generated the popular use of light therapy for healing. Even stylists note the impact of color on runway models and upwardly mobile professionals. Hypnosis has become hypnotherapy and promises to replace step-by-step psychological analysis with exponential, breakthrough possibilities.

Sometimes our light goes out, but is blown into flame by another human being. Each of us owes deepest thanks to those who have rekindled this light.
Albert Schweitzer

Chapter 9
Orderly Altered States

The eternal is all possibility. Quantum physicists speculate that reality is information and energy in a void of all possible states of energy and information. In other words, anything is possible. God is the source of this field of all possibilities. Humans play in this field. When you begin to regard your activities in the quantum field as play, you allow yourselves to release beliefs and actions you no longer need and engage new activities.

Quantum knowledge is useful for dismantling as well as creating. When you hit a "brick wall," or when life seems a series of stop signs; you can employ quantum thought. These blocks, though they seem rigid, are simply states of information and energy that either you formed or others formed around you. Perhaps theses thoughts were constructed out of fear, or unconscious motives. However they manifest in your lives, they feel real. Dismantling, or as I like to term it, dissolving these blocks sometimes requires professional assistance. Yet sometimes it only requires a nice bath of sea salts or a trip to the ocean.

When you get the blues or feel what alcoholics refer to as the hole in the center of our souls that only God can fill, you are experiencing states of energy and information. Collections of beliefs and accumulated actions form these depressive states. There's nothing like being single at a date movie to send you "home alone." There's nothing like an inflated housing market to make you question your decision to rent. There's nothing like seeing an MTV chick with a great body and a ring of admirers, to make your circle of friends shrink and your apartment feel grungy. Disconnected, isolated, and pathetic are just a few of the packets of information and energy we assume from the playground of life.

Yet, these states exist within all possible energy and information. These states exist in an absolute field of all possibilities. Realizing this scientific fact, it is easy to release disconnection, isolation and pathetic states and replace them with connection, inclusion and success. Then, you can begin to collect new information and energy states around new possibilities. You literally create your reality. Neither the dismantling nor the creation happens instantly. Both seem to occur in stages. There is a gentle, gradual movement away from and toward another reality.

The trick is not complicating the playground. Newtonian science with its minute measurement and addiction to quantitative proof and scientific method removed the magic from life. Until finally, quantum physics waved its magic wand and offered the reality of ease. Some liken dismantling to peeling an onion. Layer after layer releases. Our creation unfolds like a work of art—gradually and beautifully. One brush stroke after the next. One more spin on the potter's wheel and then into the kiln. One day you realize a part of your life is a finished art form. The release is over; a new you emerges.

After eleven years of raising my children as single parent, I finally sensed that my family was a completed work of art. Weddings, grandchildren, and planning my last child's college graduation triggered the feeling of completion. Magically, the anxiety, worry, fear, and burdens lessened. My parenting work in progress was complete. While we would always possess strong, powerful family ties, it was now time for them to each form their own families. Our shared experiences through divorce and alcoholism formed a multi-ringed trunk marked with memory and supported by a deep abiding, sustaining root system. Now it was time for each child to branch off. Now it was time for a part of me to emerge into the quantum field to create new dimensions in my life.

Hypnosis, as a tool used to enhance life, highlights the workings of the quantum field. As a hypnotherapist, I witness the ease of clients breathing and relaxing into life changes. My office space is comfortable and serene. Sessions may last up to two hours. Initially, the client shares as I actively listen and ask questions for clarity. Establishing the client's presenting issue, I then discuss hypnosis techniques. If the client wishes, under hypnosis they gradually calm their conscious mind, allowing their unconscious mind to communicate. The unconscious dwells in the eternal, absolute field of all possibilities. It wants only our highest good. It is free from accumulated sludge of the conscious mind. And freed it can easily remove the blocks, fears, prejudices, and judgments—allowing our highest, best self to emerge.

Now, this emerging higher self may come as a surprise. It did for me. As part of my training in hypnotherapy, I decided to commit to personal hypnotherapy sessions. I believed an effective hypnotherapist needed first-hand experience. Initially my hypnotherapy sessions felt like a trawler, cutting through blocks of ice on an Arctic passage. I released life experiences that were literally frozen, encased in blocks of ice. Gradually, one after the other, the thought forms melted and released. Then buried memories emerged—abuse, sorrow, physical pain, bondage, depression. On some level, I always knew the memories were there. So it wasn't a complete surprise.

The surprise was the ease in which I then released the painful memories. Like blowing the seeds from a dying dandelion, a mere whispered breath and they flew from my mind and body. The memories did not attack me or harm me or send me into a psychotic state—they simply disappeared and dissolved. And as they disappeared and dissolved they "just became memories." Their power was unplugged from my conscious and unconscious mind. They were like a song, a lyric that floated up and out of me.

My hypnotherapist and I cleaned my psychic closet. We rearranged what I wanted to keep and discarded the rest. I donated those discarded thought forms to the "Goodwill" of the universe. I thanked them and blessed them as they dissolved.

Then my hypnotherapist began to guide me by asking powerful questions. Together, we traveled into a heightened sphere where I connected with the states of energy and information present when I came into this earth life. I was surrounded by an ethereal light—opalescent, pink, blue, white. Familiar energies swirled around me. Then other figures appeared, first a female with Mary energy—Magdalene or Mother Mary. Then a male figure, one who seemed to radiate DeMolay, *Templar* energy. The Mary energy communicated that I came into this earth plane to bring extraterrestrial, multi-dimensional information into the religious community and culture.

I was taken aback. This was not exactly the assignment I wanted. My conscious mind invaded the experience—it is never totally silent. I voiced reservations about communicating to religious groups. I knew their apprehensions and beliefs regarding extraterrestrial knowledge. It was a tough assignment. The spirit simply smiled. Yes, that is one of the groups you are to work with. The ET, inter-dimensional assignment seemed easier. I was already on the path of hypnotherapy training and anomalous phenomenon study with Dr. Ruth Hover. ET energy was manifesting in my life. I liked its energy.

The hypnotherapy sessions ended, but the openings were just beginning. I was on a parallel two-track knowledge train. Ancient religious texts appeared in my email. Unsolicited, my friends emailed complete translations of Gnostic texts. I read the Nag Hammadi. Laurence Gardner and Margaret Starbird shared information of the Magdalene. I uncovered ancient foundations of the Ten Commandments and Proverbs as re-worked Egyptian documents. I discovered ancient Mesopotamian Messiah myths integrated into stories of Jesus. My mind cherished the new found jewels of wisdom once discarded by the canonized biblical tradition.

My theological education emphasized the Germanic search for the historical Jesus more than doctrine and discipline. So, these ancient sources banned from the canon of the Bible were no surprise. In the past, I had not paid much attention to their presence. Now their presence took on new meaning.

Templar information was also familiar; only now, online sources and a plethora of books provided a comprehensive history. The Cathars, the pure ones, the bloodline of the family of Jesus, the treasures smuggled from beneath Solomon's Temple came alive through Templar history. Like Templar researchers, I felt the weight of the importance of this historical era and its resultant pools of resources, knowledge, and connections that continue to infuse our culture. Templar knowledge acted like stones dropped in the human pool of knowledge, rippling ever outward. Despite DeMolay's sacrificial death, Templar knowledge didn't die. The inquisition didn't end their reign, like reptilians, they moved underground.

Without exception, every megalithic monument is in a certain relationship with subterranean currents which pass, cross or surround them.
Louis Merle and Charles Diot

Chapter 10
Vessel Vine and Vision

Certain puzzles are never solved. Templar and Gnostic sources felt like dense, tropical foliage, wet and heavy with information. Their information occupied a metaphysical realm that spanned generations searching for the key to the philosopher's stone or Jason's mythical quest for the Golden Fleece. Metaphysical wisdom packaged in an idiosyncratic form. The search never ends.

In the past I embarked on intellectual journeys, consuming each and every text, follow each and every tangent. This time it was different. Calm settled over my mind. This material felt familiar. There was no need to rush, push, or compulsively attack— information would unfold. This information had a life of its own. I was more than a searcher. I was a participant.

I learned to read with my quantum mind. At some unconscious, sub-atomic level I felt one with the information. I simply needed to open my conscious mind to accept the hidden resources. It wasn't about a mad chase. It was about a calm, easy, confident opening.

Did my reality shift as I accumulated new information and formed new perspectives? Yes. Realities are like attachments to loved ones. You are adept at making connections. Attachments create realities— your beliefs, family, friends, physical body. For a time they fill your consciousness vessel, defining who you are. Then, new information is presented and our vessel empties as we question and reconsider. Then, as new information integrates, you make new attachments. Your consciousness vessel is capable of holding waves of beliefs that ebb and flow. It is a matter of choosing or giving yourself permission. Of course, powerful existing attachments may rebel at your audacity to question or resist their pull. That is part of the process of emptying consciousness to allow new information.

Familiar attachments may not release with ease. They may clamor for yet one more tie, yet one more obligation. They may make another stab at our guilt or threaten punishment. And so, gently remove each attachment you are ready to release, thank it for the wisdom it has bestowed in your life and release it to move on. Releasing conscious attachments is loving, attentive, non-judgmental work.

Then the process of filling your vessel starts again. When Western religion lost the Magdalene, we lost awareness of part of our essential human nature. With the loss of the Magdalene, we also lost awareness of the workings of our human consciousness. We are consciousness vessels, filling with information, beliefs, and attachments. Questioning and evolving, then emptying. Lying fallow for a time in the void. Then refilling and reordering. Through this process our human consciousness awakens a new self.

Holy Communion and sharing in the story of the crucifixion and resurrection of Jesus Christ is the primary vessel image in Western Christianity. In that biblical story, vessel is about blood and wine, suffering, death, and resurrection. It is a rather violent story. In comparison, with the Magdalene as a holy vessel, we get to the same junction of resurrection and new life with less suffering and drama. The difference is in the details of the journey. Magdalene is nurturing, female, filling, and then emptying. She is the birth process without the pain. She is the resurrection without the suffering. She is the acknowledgement of simple, easy, natural human transformation.

Yet, we all need and desire different stories. And that is okay. As your journey progresses you adopt different stories to meet different needs and awareness. Today, I rarely use the word "truth." Instead I substitute the word reality. Try it. Each time you want to declare something as "truth," use the word "reality." Suddenly your belief is not so irrefutable. Suddenly you are not setting up a conflict of ideas. Instead, you are simply referring to the body of beliefs and attachments that fill your vessel...now. And, by using the term "reality" you affirm that those beliefs may change. With this word transfer, others are granted freedom to accept or reject your current vessel of ideas. If they reject it, no loss. Your vessel remains. If they accept it, no gain. Your vessel remains.

As the contents of my consciousness vessel emptied, individuals filled my life bringing new perspectives. Dr. Ruth asked me to staff Chet and Kallista Snow's Signs of Destiny Conference in Tempe, Arizona. Year after year, I staffed the registration table, and became acquainted with the conference participants, presenters, and information. The conference focused on **Crop Circle** research, bringing together an international community of researchers, scientists, and scholars, dedicated to solving the riddles in the fields. Scientists like Nancy Talbot explained the laser-like phenomenon present in crop circles. The actual physical nature of the stem was affected as the circle formed. Changes in the crops were not the result of being smashed with wooden boards; there was a visible change. Scientific research proved the authenticity of the phenomenon.

Along with scientists, metaphysical researchers provided another world of information within the circles. They introduced ancient arts into a technological, scientific dialogue. What were the circles communicating? You needed ancient eyes to see. The Signs of Destiny conference discussion blended science and religion, technology, and metaphysics to research a phenomenon that is as beautiful as it is mystifying.

Metaphysical researchers employed the ancient art of ***numerology*** and geometrics—making a detailed count of each angle, row, and shape in the circles. They sighted the circle in relation to sacred landmarks. They explored how year after year, similar shapes evolve and grow in complexity. It was as if, over a span of years, certain shapes communicated more information by replicating and enhancing shapes. Over the years, a simple form grew complex and multifaceted. Crop circle forms taught us to read an ancient language, using symbols, numbers, and shape. Sitting in the dark auditorium, watching one crop circle slide after the next, new understanding unfolded. My quantum mind connected. At some level of consciousness, I could read symbols, numbers, and shapes. Like a child fed monosyllabic sounds, I eventually learned the language. I created words and linguistics emerged. Somewhere in my consciousness, connections grew. Neurologically, crop circle symbolic language awakened brain networks. I could read. I could communicate.

Crop circle researchers provided additional ancient connections. They consulted the numerology of ancient civilizations—Mayan, Aztec, Egyptian, Greek, Sumerian, Hebrew. Numbers often lead to an apocalyptic forecast, an end of time prediction. Numbers alerted us that something was going to happen, or was happening. My theological background made me wary of timed predictions. Whether predictions of wars, pestilence, climate chaos, or the return of the Messiah; I understood the religious predilection to apocalypse. Early Christians spent their lives waiting for a physical return of their messiah.

Individuals today spend their lives plotting the advent of 2012. I reacted to apocalyptic predictions with a red flag. Tread carefully.

Time is not what we imagine—past, present, or future. Events are not what we imagine. Events occur in multiple dimensions—conscious, unconscious, dimensional. Yet, crop circle messages and Mayan history pointed to a transformative reality. Could the apocalyptic forecast of the crop circles simply be a means of marking the possible transitions of human consciousness and physical form? Our way out—or our way in—to another era, another reality? As I viewed the crop circles and connected with ancient knowledge I became aware of my shift in consciousness. Crop circle language filled my vessel with new information that spawned new beliefs and a new reality.

Metaphysical numbers were fascinating. They signaled beginnings, endings, and periods of transitions. When an experience is blessed with meaningful numbers, it sends a message that all is well. I am in sync with nature and life in all its dimensions.

For me, the number nine is particularly meaningful. It signals fruition and completion. The end of an era. They send a signal to our consciousness that it is time to release and let go of certain belief attachments. We can follow the path of release opened by the number. Or we can deny its reality. Either way works. Yet, when it feels like it is time for your consciousness to shift and new experiences and information to emerge, then numbers can be your guide.

A dear friend, who separated and divorced from her beloved husband, taught me the meaning of nine as completion and release. After nine years together, she chose to end and complete her marriage relationship with love and compassion. Amid the inevitable sorrow, guilt, regret, and anger of divorce, she held a space in her heart and mind filled with understanding, compassion and trust. In this space, human feelings were not denied, they were encouraged to gain expression and then tenderly loved and released. Laughter and lightness of being filled the dark crevices. Watching humorous movies together or taking a walk broke the back of anger and ugly silences. The spine of the former relationship transformed into a supple muscle that could release and move on. Through divorce she developed the spine of a compassionate master.

Three is another meaningful number. It has caused some amazing historical divisions and harmony. The doctrine of the trinity separated Eastern Orthodox and Western Christianity. Was there an historical disagreement or was the disagreement a red herring? Was the disagreement hubbub masking another important issue? Perhaps the important issue was whether the seat of religion would be in Rome or Constantinople. It was a political conflict, dressed in the heavy, moralistic garb of religion. To emphasize its importance it was further draped in holy numbers (3) and names. Today, no one cares or even remembers the disagreement, except religious historians. It is a non-issue.

Yet, talking about the power and presence of God seems to require the number three. God, Father, Holy Spirit. There is completion in three. Three deaths are a complete cycle according to superstitions. Experts in marketing claim that a client needs to hear your name three times before they connect with you.

Symbolically, I biologically birthed three children. As I was leaving my Scottsdale home and moving into a condo, I received messages about three stones. Somehow three stones were important in my life. For years I contemplated the meaning of three stones and looked for their appearance. Since I live in a rock-strewn desert, there were plenty of opportunities. Yet, none pointed to anything meaningful. Now, I realize that the three stones were my children and that I was to tend to their welfare. Three. Simple number. Powerful number.

Not only was the number meaningful, so was the object. Stones or rocks possess dense, compact meaning. Jesus said he, or his message was the rock. Ancients believed that stones held the wisdom of the Earth. Peter founded the church upon a rock. He founded the church upon the wisdom of the Earth. Jerusalem and the Dome of the Rock are sacred sites built upon the wisdom of the Earth.

At my mother's memorial, the minister shared her wisdom about child rearing. She believed that you could teach your children, hoping they would learn. Then you released them into the world. The world then became their teacher. World lessons may be difficult and harsh, but they will learn.

My children carried wisdom lessons of my Earth life. Raising them, I was to learn the ways of the Earth. Our experience would refine my knowledge, grinding away apprehensions and mistaken beliefs. My children were my portals to become a functioning earthling. The lessons from those three stones are too numerous to list. One important lesson was trust. Bankrupt, home foreclosed, earning barely enough money to get by—somehow day after day we managed and thrived. Bills were paid. Insurance was secured. Cars were purchased and repaired. Clothing was bought. High school, college, graduate schools completed. How did the money manifest? Each day I journaled, sometimes making detailed lists of what I needed. Each and every need was fulfilled. Each and every one.

Do I still forget to trust the fulfillment of all of my needs and begin to panic? Of course. Then I relax and remember. Life is a field of limitless possibilities. I play in the field; I do not own the field. Each and every moment of your Earth life, you can choose to live in fields of wealth, health, beauty and happiness. You are privileged to call these rich veins of Earth, your home.

My three children taught me the core strengths of love. We came from an alcoholic, abusive environment where walls echoed screams and tantrums. The illness of alcoholism invaded all our psychics. When I closed the door to my Scottsdale home and opened the door to my condo, I chose a new way of communicating. I chose to speak slowly, gently, and calmly to my children. Frightened, they flew into tantrums. Fearful, they resorted to familiar angry outbursts. Each and every time, I responded in a quiet, calm voice. With time, waves of anger subsided. With time, fear withdrew. Every spoken word of peace and love formed a foundational building block.

Our transformation of anger into love reminded me of classic Earth behavior. In Hawaii, tide pools are formed by the angry, red-hot lava flow. In the gentle arms of the ocean, hot lava flows transform into safe tide pools filled with children splashing and swimming. Angry lava forms safe cocoons on the shores of a vast ocean. As our words to one another soften, as our actions become gentle and loving, hot anger transforms into tide pools. Our family now floats in a protected tide pool. Together we created a lagoon. With my three stones I built a home.

Emptying Exercise

Benefits of Exercise:

- Ease of detachment
- Remove, release, and resolve all you no longer need

Do you feel it is time to release an attachment or belief that no longer serves you? When it is time—numbers, symbols, animals, and visions will come. Trust them. They open your path.

If possible, correlate the timing of your release with the tides of the universe. The waxing and waning of the moon is a power ally. After the moon is full and then begins to wane, is a powerful time for letting go. As the moon releases, so do you.

There are many ways to release. I release by writing. You may release by crying or dancing or singing. Choose your release. There is no right or wrong way to release. On a full moon I journal the attachment I am releasing. I write until I am clear.

Then I determine the new thoughts and beliefs I want use to fill my mind, replacing the old attachments. I write the new beliefs as affirmations. "I am..." statements. I write until the affirmations are simple and clear. Next, I set the intention that my new belief and the responsive sift in my consciousness come easily and effortlessly. I allow them to unfold.

On the full moon, I go into my body and become aware of my cellular memory where I physically carry the old beliefs and attachments. I move gently up and down my body, identifying places where I store these old beliefs. As you move up and down your body, you will notice a stronger vibration in one area. This is your cellular storehouse. This is the area you need to clean—remove, release and resolve.

At each location of a cellular storehouse in your body, first take time to honor the presence of the attachment. Thank it for being in your body and for the wisdom it gave. Next, communicate to the storehouse that you will be removing the attachment.

Then gently and easily, gather all the tentacles of the belief or attachment from your storehouse. This is similar to what happens when you remove a program from your computer. The computer knows how to go through every file and collect all the attachments from the program you are removing. When all your attachments are gathered, collect them with an imaginary hand, and gently pull them from your body's storehouse. As you pull them out, repeat that you completely remove, release, and resolve the attachment. Dispose of the attachment in any way you choose. Toss it, burn it, bury it.

Then, in the final act, return to the physical site of the attachment storehouse. Fill the cellular storehouse with light and love. Allow your thoughts to bring a vibration of health, peace, and love into the storehouse. This light sparks the fire of transformation.

Throughout the following days, if the old attachment resurfaces, simply become aware of breathing and repeat your affirmation. This repetitive anchoring of your intention is similar to the alcoholics' phrase that you "fake it until you make it." Retraining your mind with new affirmations is important, easy, and effective. With each day, the need to retrain will lessen.

If you draw a circle in the sand and study only what's inside the circle, then that is a closed-system perspective. If you study what is inside the circle and everything outside the circle, then that is an open system perspective.
Buckminster Fuller

CHAPTER 11
CONSCIOUSNESS CRAFT

Consciousness is corded. Through exploring human consciousness I experienced a direct link to the Earth, the underworld, and the cosmos. Inter-dimensional and extra-dimensional consciousness. I experienced how consciousness cords could be used to travel, learn, and communicate. You, too, can use these cosmic cords to explore multiple dimensions and evolve as a galactic being. The vision inspired by Jamie Maussan's video, the possibility of humans possessing a consciousness craft, can become your reality.

Yet, first we need to examine human consciousness. It is the key. The study of consciousness is an experiential and also an academic endeavor. The following consciousness discussion is somewhat academic. I made it an easy read. Take time to enjoy it and then apply it to your experience.

Throughout Western history, humans defined consciousness by developing models of the mind based on functions of the brain. Often these models reflected inventions and cultural threads of thought. In early Alexandria culture, Galen (AD130-200), an anatomist, examined the brain and determined it to be filled with empty spaces, called ventricles. He determined these empty spaces were filled with a gaseous, ethereal substance inhaled from the cosmos. This ethereal substance that filled empty spaces of the brain was called spirit (Illing, 2004).

Later in history, the mind was imaged as a fountain with an animating spirit that flowed through its spaces. Descarte (1596-1650), who solidified the separation of mind and body, perceived the brain as similar to a pipe organ, moving air through a complex array of heart and arteries. Freud (1856-1939) perceived the mind as similar to a hydraulic system or steam engine. It is interesting that the steam engine was invented during his lifetime. The stem of the mind, of course, was desire and sexual impulse. Nice analogy, Doctor.

In the 20th Century, behaviorists saw the brain as a sophisticated telephone switchboard, again relying on technological inventions. In their model, memory was a matter of setting up internal switches. When signals were properly routed, then actions were easily performed. Post WW II, engineers developed *Cybernetics*, which posited that information was the attribute of an interaction between subjective and objective. They perceived a holistic model of the mind as an organism. The field of Artificial Intelligence is dedicated to developing intelligent machines. As such, they often view the human brain as a computer. As quantum computing advances, they integrate it into technological models of the mind.

So, where are we today? Any further along than Freud or Cybernetics? Was there a consensus in the definition of consciousness? Unfortunately, no. Finding an agreed upon definition of consciousness proved elusive. Maybe that was because consciousness studies are subjective as well as objective. I found that consciousness studies, though ancient, had only recently, in the 1990s, been accepted into the academic university curriculum. In current consciousness studies, biologists researching the neurological workings of the brain joined with mathematicians postulating quantum theories. These experts united with philosophers eager to move beyond dualism and perhaps even resurrect Platonic ideals more amenable to quantum science. As these academics dialogued, a definitive, consensual definition of consciousness dissolved. Academic waters muddied, though they may soon clear.

Common definitions of consciousness often refer to its opposite, the unconscious. One who is conscious is awake and alert. One who is unconsciousness is in an altered state, either chemically or sleep induced. Susan Blackmore, in her book, *Consciousness: An introduction,* molded consciousness studies into a textbook based curriculum. She defines consciousness as "knowing something, or attending to something" (p.5). It is the equivalent of subjectivity, the first person view of the world. Consciousness doesn't fit neatly into brain studies or biological definitions. She boldly asserts, "studying consciousness will change your life" (p.5). One is left wondering whether her consciousness assertion includes changing your scientific theories and academic assumptions.

Others, such as Leslie Brothers, a psychiatrist, question whether consciousness is an entity or a thing. Is it only a concept? Stuart Hameroff, an anesthesiologist, who handles patient consciousness on a daily basis, asserts that consciousness in a restrictive sense is experience. It is an awareness possessed by biological systems. Joe Bogen, neurosurgeon, maintains that the brain produces consciousness. He looks at levels— subcellular, cytoskeleton, microtubles, cellular, circuit levels, as well as how one brain interacts with others. Agreement is scarce. Disagreement is the consensus (Kuhn, 2005).

At a Tucson Conference in 1994, philosopher David Chalmers pulled the consciousness discussion toward what he defined as the "hard problem" and the "easy problem". The easy consciousness problems were not solved, but we are making progress. The easy problems included the brain's ability to discriminate, categorize, and react to environmental stimuli; integrate information; report on its own mental states; focus attention; and exert deliberate control over behavior. The hard problem was determining how standard physiological processes translate to subjective experience (Huff, 2005). What is it like to be a biological organism? What is it like to be in a given mental state? The thorny philosophical mind body issues were once again on stage and experience the star as the hard problem.

The media weighed in on the hard problem and speculated in movies such as *Matrix* (1999) that evil computer aliens imposed a version of reality on humans from the outside. Chalmers seems to question the scriptwriter's fantasy. Instead, he theorizes that the brain appears to be constructing reality from within on the fly as waves of sensory information flood from the outer world. He marvels at how our brain processes a tsunami of sensory data (Huff, 2005). Our brain's involvement is essential.

In *Wider than the Sky: The Phenomenal Gift of Consciousness*, 1972 Nobel Prize winning neuroscientist, Gerald Edelman uses magnetoencephalography, a non-invasive technique, to explain the workings of our brain. He measured tiny electromagnetic currents in small groups of neurons to develop neurological correlates of consciousness. He determined that there is no one place in the brain where consciousness takes place. No command center. There is also a wide variation in neural response among individuals responding to the same stimulus or scene. Finally he determines that the brain or the mind is not "software." He agrees with William James, "thoughts don't necessarily need a thinker." His research points to the possibility that our working brain was not designed, but evolved, as he postulates a "neural Darwinism"(O'Reilly, 2005).

The promising model of anesthesiologist Hameroff and mathematician Penrose proposes that quantum computation occurs in *cytoskeletal microtubles* within the brain's neurons. "The basic idea is that consciousness involves brain activities compiled to self-organizing ripples in fundamental reality. Brain stimulates reality based on sensory input and is also intimately connected to that reality at the quantum level" (Huff, 2005).

What about cosmic consciousness as the evil alien computers? Is it a media parody of reality at the quantum level? "In Panpsychism theory, mind is fundamental in the universe. All matter has associated mental aspects or properties.... Everything in the universe is seen as conscious" (Blackmore, 2004. p.11). Critics of panpsychism question why are there both physical and mental properties. This criticism is another door that leads to the hard problem. But Chalmers indicates that the door must be opened. At the 1994 Tucson conference, he claimed that consciousness was a fundamental constituent of reality. It may be a building block of the universe, as photons are to light. Consciousness may be an inherent requirement of all that surrounds and composes us (Huff, 2005).

Is the evil alien computer simply a means of imaging consciousness at the quantum level, albeit a fearful image? Physicists, neurosurgeons, philosophers, and mathematicians substitute the less threatening term ***proto-consciousness*** to indicate that consciousness may be a fundamental constituent of reality, a building block. Is this a spiritual force? Danah Zohar (2001) merges religion and science with proto-consciousness. In her book *SQ: Connecting with our Spiritual Intelligence*, she writes that David Chalmers found the following:

> proto-consciousness is a fundamental property of all matter, just like mass, charge, spin, and location. In this view, proto-consciousness is a natural part of the fundamental physical laws of the universe and has been present since the beginning of time. Everything that exists—fundamental particles like mesons and quarks, atoms, stones, tree trunks...possess proto-consciousness. (p.81)

Is proto-consciousness the universal "mud" where Buddhists image the stem of the lotus rooting, emerging to flower as individual spiritual path? Are we all rooted in proto-consciousness and emerge from the stem of creation to follow our designated spiritual paths this lifetime? Zohar agrees, "If neural oscillations in the brain were a coherent version of a fundamental property pervading the whole universe, then our human SQ roots us not just in life but at the very heart of the universe. We become children, not just of life, but of the cosmos" (Zohar, 2001, p. 82).

Proto-consciousness, the mud of consciousness, may also be the answer to riddles of string theory. According the Michio Kaku, string theory was stumbling over the possibility of a world hidden from our senses. Quantum theory made it impossible to pinpoint the exact location of atomic particles like electrons. They had no single location. Subatomic worlds operated by outlandish laws that called into question many scientific theories. Kaku began to solve the riddle of subatomic worlds by positing the possibility of parallel worlds. He identified the difficulties of merging string theory and cosmological concepts like the big bang. The laws of string theory physics break down with the big bang. String theory formulas failed to work with the big bang theory. Then a once dismissed theory of super gravity re-emerged with an elegant 11-string theory. After years of being dismissed by the string theorists, the super gravity model of 11 strings offered hope. "The astonishing conclusion was that all the matter in the Universe was connected to one vast structure: a membrane. The quest to explain everything in the Universe could begin again and at its heart would be this new theory. It was dubbed ***Membrane Theory*** or M Theory" (Barlow, 2002).

In the super gravity model, gravity was noted as extremely weak in comparison with other forces. They questioned whether this weakness was because gravity was leaking from our universe. Then the question was flipped, what if gravity was in fact leaking into our universe from another universe, perhaps a parallel universe. Membrane Theory and 11 string dimensions indicated it was so.

How does consciousness fit in Membrane Theory? If mathematicians could work with the force of gravity to develop formulas to fit Membrane Theory, what about the nature of consciousness? *Was consciousness leaking out of our brains? Or was consciousness leaking in from a membrane into our brains and bodies?* Was M theory, mother theory? Were our prehistoric matrilineal ancestors on to a significant cosmic fact that we moderns have overlooked? Might our culture be preparing to re-embrace the Great Mother? Was the evil alien computer really a nurturing great mother—Kwan Yin, Magdalene, Mother Mary, Isis, Mother of the Universe?

Consciousness research, like a secret code, stimulates an intellectual desire to solve the puzzle. Our minds innately desire closure—problem solved. Yet, consciousness research is a boundless frontier. One theory spawns multiple questions. And yet, being human, the search to quantify, classify, comprehend, and use consciousness takes precedence. Regardless of the thicket of criticism, the image models made passé by science and technology, the subjective trump card, humans are conscious beings. We want to know who we are.

Through research and learning, your consciousness expands. New vistas and possibilities form. Research and theories beget the development of consciousness. The search is eternal.

Exoconscious Ufology

A college-student relates a story of night communication with an extraterrestrial. A scientist explains he has been in contact with grays since childhood. A pilot recounts a vast extraterrestrial craft paralleling his jet and his reluctance to make a formal report. A former army intelligence officer finally testifies to a secret career in alien crash retrieval.

Who are you to believe? How can you test or validate individual experience? Are these witnesses imagining encounters or are they real-time events? The sheer number of contact testimonies, like the sheer number of craft sightings, demands attention, examination, and validation. To accomplish this, ufology needs exoconsciousness.

The foundation of exoconsciousness was developed by Harvard anomalous researcher and psychiatrist, John Mack. He termed his work with contact experiencers "legitimizing the witness." He sought a compatible scientific framework to give voice and structure to a reality beyond the common daily conscious experience. I honor his legacy with exoconsciousness.

"Legitimizing the witness" highlights the experiencer phenomenon of consciousness to consciousness contact between humans and other-dimensional beings. It validates the possibility of a relationship between intelligent beings from differing realities. It authenticates the possibility of communicating an experience beyond language, opening the door of symbol, myth, mathematics. It opens the possibility of enhanced human linguistic abilities and creation of a new language. It pushes the envelope of human conscious abilities into a frontier where we develop skills and abilities once thought the stuff of science fiction, now becoming reality.

"Legitimizing the witness" is not a new struggle. Religious, spiritual, and metaphysical testimonies are fraught with the inability of witnesses to communicate their experience. Prophets, mediums, clairvoyants, and intuitives hone a repertoire of skills beyond the 3R's of classical education. Altered states of consciousness are common in religion, spirituality, and metaphysics. Switch on any religious network and witness the swaying, chanting, repetitive, hypnotic music that nurtures the believers. Click on any Buddhist or New Age website and witness the step-by-step instruction toward an altered state of consciousness into the bliss of oneness. Open a classical metaphysical text and read the formulated concoctions for transcendence. Exoconsciousness, utilizing extraterrestrial dimensions of our human consciousness, to communicate, travel, and create inter-dimensionally is simply a current description of altered states.

While religion and philosophy struggle with "legitimizing the witness", they also provide a rich background for understanding consciousness. Classical theology approached consciousness through the doorways of moral theology and concepts such as the soul. They searched for a means to understand eternity glimpsed by humans. Then through Newtonian science, criticism and analysis, they pulled apart mind from body. They relegated the body as an earthly being and the mind as connected to a possible soul or eternity.

In an attempt to distinguish humans from other life forms, classical theologians concentrated on free will and the ability to conceptualize. Eventually they formulated human free will into structured church doctrine. Human volition, seen as one of the primary features separating humans and animals, was a powerful force that could be used for good and evil. So a hierarchical doctrine was composed as a means of controlling human freewill. It was perceived as divine…but…well not really. Freewill needed structure and control. Philosophers and theologians still struggle with the human ability to pick and choose, to create experiences and to exercise freewill. The ancient scholars chose freewill as the distinguishing trait of humanness. And this trait has caused no end of academic difficulty. Was freewill a poor choice?

To understand conscious behavior, prior to scientific experimentation and technology, philosophers and theologians began a detailed, (sometimes convoluted) inductive analysis of mental states. Socratic and Platonic philosophers commenced the allegorical examination of the conscious mind comparing it to shadows in a cave, where the shadows represented created illusions. Neo-platonic philosophers such as Hegel, continued the examination of illusion within human constructs of reality by employing a phenomenological method that bracketed experience.

To unravel the conscious mind, psychologists devised several tests to determine if an individual or animal is conscious. The Turing Test was devised to determine if computers could simulate human consciousness. In the Turing Test a judge engages two other parties—one human, the other machine-- in a natural conversation. If the judge cannot reliably tell which is which, then the machine is said to pass the Turing Test. In this case both the human and the machine appear human. In order to keep the test setting simple and universal they devised a text messaging conversation that could be used by both humans and machines. To date, the test remains controversial. Possibly the evolved ability to text message while driving gives humans an edge in the competition.

The Mirror Test developed by Gordon Gallup, was based on whether or not animals were able to recognize themselves in a mirror as a baseline for consciousness. According to the test, 18 month-old humans, some apes, and bottlenose dolphins indicated self-recognition consciousness.

The Delay Test focused on the delay between stimulus and response as a means of separating instinctual/reflexive response from determined conscious choice or involvement.

Freud and classical psychologists, rooted in science, philosophy, and religion brought a new framework to understanding consciousness. They provided the language and experimentation to understand the various levels of consciousness—subconscious, unconscious, conscious mind. From there modern psi-researchers such as William James, J.B.

Rhine, and the contemporary researcher, Dean Radin, provide essential information about para-psychic abilities.

Moving into the 21st Century, we considered the research of Hammeroff, Penrose, and Chalmers that integrated quantum science with consciousness research. The consciousness theories of Hammeroff, Penrose, and Chalmers would not be possible without the accompanying scientific breakthrough.

Are contemporary consciousness theories integrating quantum theories and computer science any more valid or reliable than Freud's comparison of the brain to a steam engine? If so, like the chicken and egg—which comes first: human consciousness theories or technological inventions? Or are they both human constructs, one mental, one physical?

...there will be no total disclosure anytime soon.
The ETs are doing this on a one-on-one basis.
John Lear

CHAPTER 12
DNA MOTHER SHIP

Innovation initiates new states of consciousness. Alternative healing provides a platform for the use of expanded consciousness. Both the patient and the practitioner are involved in using states of consciousness for healing. Extraterrestrial reality and the development of exoconsciousness are closely tied to the experience and acceptance of alternative healing. Alternative healing is **homeopathic** and Western medicine is **allopathic**.

Allopathic medicine is traditional western medical treatment in which multiple drugs are used to treat multiple symptoms. For example, a prescription for the flu would incorporate drugs for relief of fever, aches, and sleeplessness, as well as drugs to attack the flu virus. Traditional physicians and health practitioners—doctors, nurses, psychiatrists—use allopathic medicine.

Homeopathic medicine originated through the work of a 19th Century German physician, Samuel Christian Hahnemann. It is based on three primary laws: similars, single remedy, and minimum doses. The law of similars is termed "the hair of the dog." Homeopathic medicine prescribes natural herbal medicine that creates similar symptoms to what the patient is experiencing in their illness. A thorough exploration of symptoms is done by the homeopathic practitioner. The law of single remedy is the belief that a single medicine covers all symptoms. An underlying belief in homeopathy is that there is a plant extract available that has a perfectly matched frequency to the illness. The third law is minimum doses. Small, sometime infinitesimal doses are prescribed. Then the physician waits to observe the effect.

Many forms of natural healing are now mainstream. Natural healing is based on the assumption that the body's innate healing ability can be triggered to create health. Natural healing includes sound, color, and word healing protocols. These practices are based on providing the most effective healing frequency for the illness. Other healing practices that align with the natural energy pathways of the body to speed healing include ayurveda, acupuncture, qigong; spiritual healings such as **Reiki** and **Johrei,** as well as mind-based healing such as hypnotherapy and coaching.

Alternative healing is a field with many practitioners, many approaches. In alternative medicine, individuals are free to choose the modality most effective for their particular circumstance and needs. Unlike allopathic or western medicine, there are no pharmaceutical prescriptions, strict protocols, or closed systems. Certainly each practitioner is trained in specific protocols and develops allegiance to particular healing tools. As an alternative system, it will always be an open system--open to the evolving needs of clients, open to cutting edge research. Alternative healing is the perfect complement to allopathic, western medicine.

Most alternative healing is non-invasive, gentle, and powerful. What could be gentler than a Reiki master sending healing light energy into your body? What could be less invasive than receiving distant Reiki from a group of healers united by the internet across the world? What could be more cutting edge than Johrei light energy transmitted by a healer holding the palm of their hands over the crown of your head?

What could be more powerful than an energy worker who realigns your entire energy field?

Alternative healers work in the realm of subtle energy fields, harnessing the power of the body to heal. They make a commitment to continuous clarity in order to transmit pure light. To accomplish this they make another commitment to continuous clearing and cleansing. They make a commitment to individualize and customize each treatment to address the client's needs.

Both alternative healing and exoconsciousness operate in the sensory realm of subtle energies. Our body's subtle energy systems are experienced through the chakras, meridians, as well as the astral body. Remember the Egyptian reference to the astral body as it traveled the underworld to the stars? This astral body is superimposed and integrated with our physical body. It has a higher, broader spectrum of frequencies. Our five senses enable our physical body to operate in the world of five senses: sight, sound, taste, touch, and smell. In comparison, the astral uses psychic senses like telepathy, clairvoyance, intuition, clairsentience, and ESP. It operates on the sub-atomic, quantum level.

As my exoconsciousness developed, my community of alternative healers expanded. While not all healing communities are comfortable with extraterrestrial energies, many are open to working with them. During my hypnotherapy training our class occasionally needed to clear energies. Our instructor and assistant were vigilant about individuals coming to class clear of attached entities. Remember the exercise in chapter ten on releasing attachments? Attached entities are energies and thought forms that some define as negative because they block an individual's forward movement. Do individuals attract these negative energies to stop or slow down their movement? Yes. I believe we attract negative energies until we are ready to move on and live according to who we are, not how others perceive us. Often individuals carrying excessive negative energies can affect the learning environment of the classroom.

During one particular class, the instructor and assistant determined that every participant needed to be cleared. The participants were asked to leave. Then, one by one, we entered the classroom and stood between the instructor and assistant who cleared interfering entities and thought forms. When it was my turn, the instructor cleared unwanted attachments, and then recognized extraterrestrials surrounding me. The assistant, who was a friend and knew of my extraterrestrial work, laughed as the instructor questioned their presence. "They are always around her," she laughed. "There's no need to remove them, I'm not sure you could if you wanted to."

I took my seat with the other students and watched the clearing continue, mindful of my extraterrestrials' public appearance. It was the first of what would be numerous incidents when sensitive people recognized my connection to extraterrestrial beings. As we became friends, the assistant's interest in extraterrestrial knowledge heightened. I worked with her as she became more proficient in polarity and shamanic soul retrieval. She was always respectful of my extraterrestrial connections and together we eventually invited the extraterrestrial energies into our healing space.

Over time we became more proficient in our work, able to utilize extraterrestrial connections to quickly align energies, heal, and clear. We could telepathically communicate with our extraterrestrial partners in healing, receiving instructions and given specific protocols. My work in alternative modes of healing provided a foundation for working with extraterrestrials. Like alternative healing, the development of my exoconsciousness, the extraterrestrial dimensions of my consciousness, was non-invasive, gentle, and powerful. It centered in my subtle energy fields, and then integrated into my mental, physical, and spiritual being.

My ordinary life was imbued with an extraterrestrial dimension. I could communicate, receive, and transmit information with extraterrestrial dimensions. They were respectful, kind, and cooperative.

How did it happen? Was I lucky, fortunate, or unfortunate? The answer is simple—I asked for it to happen. Have you ever traveled to a place that resonated with the frequency of home? There you felt comfortable and secure in that particular geographic place. You had to return again and again. Regardless of where you traveled, a trip back manifested on your itinerary, until perhaps you eventually relocated there.

The sacred pull of place is similar to extraterrestrial attraction. Once I glimpsed extraterrestrial reality, I experienced a deep-rooted familiarity. Each diverse being I encountered transmitted the frequency of home. I felt an immediate comfort and security. My body resonated with knowledge that I was a star being, one with star visitors. It was as though my being carried a composite genetic makeup that magnetically drew me toward extraterrestrials. Regardless of the spiritual or metaphysical experiences, I always returned to the extraterrestrial. I am at home in extraterrestrial dimensions.

When I asked to relate to extraterrestrial beings and dimensions, I received an affirmative response. I relocated. More accurately, I bi-located. Remaining an earthling, happy and luxuriating in being human, I also live in extraterrestrial realities.

Increasingly conscious of my extraterrestrial connections and my heightened extra-sensory abilities, I began to explore how I came to be both extraterrestrial and human. Of course genetics seemed to provide the easiest answer. Wanting a simple obvious answer, I began to attract information regarding human genetic manipulation by extraterrestrials. Beyond the ancient Sumerian and Mesopotamian stories, contemporary researchers were peering into human DNA to determine our origins. Theories of extraterrestrial origins of humans raised complex questions.

Was I a hybrid—human and extraterrestrial? Did splicing extraterrestrial genes into my parents' DNA create me? If so, how and when did this happen? Had I been abducted and genetically engineered? Or had my parents? This seemed a possibility because extraterrestrials frequently referred to my bloodline. Or was I an extraterrestrial incarnation (way too theological) who manifested into a human body. Was this what Christianity referred to regarding Jesus Christ's divine incarnation into a human body? If so, was this religious story about one man or a story about the spiritual journey into the physical body of every human? That seemed more reasonable. Humans are all star incarnations.

Walk-ins posed another possibility. In Sedona, Arizona a conference attracts walk-ins. These are people who experienced another being, often an extraterrestrial, occupying their body. This could happen during a critical illness or when one momentarily died and was brought back to life. There seems to be a sliver of time when an exchange is possible. While this was not my experience, I respect that it may be a reality for others.

The issue of twin extraterrestrials also was intriguing. Do I have a twin extraterrestrial spirit who lives and breathes in me? This too was not my experience. I relate to many extraterrestrial beings, not just one. Whatever the source of cause of my extraterrestrial origins, an understanding of DNA was essential.

Conscious DNA

My human body possesses an extraterrestrial connection through my DNA and my consciousness. The human body and quantum consciousness are one. DNA answered many of my questions. DNA involved the creation of the human body. Returning to Jaimie Maussan's video of the mother ship launching and recovering the conscious craft entities, what role does the human body serve? Traditional science perceives the body as a thing, a biological, biomechanical machine that can be regulated with chemical reactions, using drugs. A valid image. Yet this image of the body falls short when related to cosmic quantum consciousness.

The valiant genome project proposes many answers in understanding the human genetic makeup while it also left the door open to flood science with new questions. The discovery and understanding of DNA forced scientists to address the issue of *junk DNA* and phantom effects. When confronted with the reality of junk DNA, the scientific manifesto, "nature is not profligate" began to sound hollow. If, as the traditional scientists speculated, nature never provides more than is needed for an organism to function in its environment, how did scientists solve the riddle of junk DNA? Junk DNA researchers argue that the majority, 97% of our DNA, does nothing (Kelleher, 1999, p.9). In this Buddhist realm of "nothingness", or unborn awareness, scientist Colm Kelleher speculated on the activity of *transposons*. According to Kelleher (1999), these useless 3 million base pairs of junk DNA await activation by retrotransposons, creating a jumping DNA phenomenon.

"Only 3% of human DNA encodes the physical body. The remaining 97% of the 3 billion base pair genome contains over a million genetic structures, called transposons, that have the capacity to jump from one chromosomal location to another. Transposons that jump to a new location via an RNA intermediate are known as retrotransposon" (Kelleher, 1999, p. 9).

According to Kelleher, there were confirmed cases of retrotransposon activation of previously unused, "read junk", DNA. This quantum-like DNA jumping phenomenon bolstered Nobel Prize winning scientist, Barbara McClintock's assumption that our genetic code or DNA was not a "static structure, transmitted unchanged generation to generation" (Kelleher, 1999, p. 11). Instead, she asserts that certain DNA sequences jump from one location to another. In other words, our genetic blueprint changes with this jumping phenomenon and Kelleher believes we are able to influence the movement.

Designing research experiments to track DNA sequence-jumping was most successful when performed as cancer research. "…it must be emphasized that in humans only the disease-causing consequences of transposition have so far been found…It is very difficult to catch an element 'in the act' of moving to a different chromosomal location" (Kelleher, 1999, p. 13).

Despite the research hurdles, Kelleher makes a bold claim and traces this activation process, or jumping DNA, to possibly explain dramatic physical conversions initiated by metaphysical or religious experience. He cites the sages, mystics, and yogis who experience age reversion, levitation, transfiguration, and possibly ascension as possibly resulting from jumping DNA. He seems to indicate that humans can somehow tap the human potential that lays dormant in our DNA and utilize it for miraculous abilities and achievements. As ancient and modern spiritual disciples have long claimed, their DNA changed (jumped) as their discipline intensified and their level of enlightenment heightened.

Awakened kundalini exemplifies another possible DNA conversion on a cellular level. Awakened disciples often comment on the feeling that every cell in their body shifts during a tantra episode of kundalini. As tantra disciple Richard Sauder writes, his body changed with an infusion of metaphysical/physical voltage:

> My spinal column was turbo-charged with what felt like 50,000 volts of rippling, crackling electricity that came surging up my spine with an ear-splitting roar and arced out of the top of my skull…my heart chakra was powerfully opened and I could see all around me without any physical impediment… the heart itself sees, with great acuity and without physical restriction, when in a state such as this (Sauder, 1998, p.11).

Could the DNA, opened through kundalini practices, be one of the paths toward cosmic consciousness? Kelleher seems to be pointing to DNA as a potential physical propellant system with which to launch a consciousness craft and then recall it back into the body. Junk DNA and the quantum-jumping phenomenon may be an energy system innate in the human body. Have generations of spiritual masters perfected this technique until the Twenty-First Century, when it may tip into the mainstream? The populated floor of yoga studios seems to indicate the path is opening.

Kenneth Ring (1989), author of *The Omega Project: Near Death Experiences, UFO Encounters and Mind at Large*, compares lengthy and spontaneous or quick enlightenment experiences. The enlightenment accessed by a lifetime discipline of a spiritual master may be the same as the dramatic, quickening of enlightenment triggered by near death experiences (NDE) and UFO encounters. Depending on the individual and the culture, the enlightenment process may be fast or slow, yet the quality of experience was similar. In a technological culture, the increasingly commonplace emergency room revival of "dead" patients provides a strong database to examine the spiritual enlightenment of NDE. This research dovetails the increasingly commonplace UFO sightings by our current culture, researched contact reports, and internet email forums as yet another database of enlightenment research.

According to the esteemed Harvard psychiatrist, John Mack (2000), who interviewed, tested, and diagnosed numerous contact experiencers, they all seemed to move through similar stages. His book, *Passport to the Cosmos: Human Transformations and Alien Encounters,* identified four dimensions accessed by the experiencers. First, each was taken against their will and given fear producing intrusive procedures. Second, upon completion and returning to everyday life, they often experienced a sense of isolation and estrangement. Third, they experienced an "ontological shock" where their normal paradigms of belief and values had to shift. They knew they were not alone in the universe. Fourth, after the paradigm shift, many seemed to manifest a spiritual enlightenment. Many experiencers interviewed and treated by Mack pushed through the terror of ***abduction*** to experience the beauty of the cosmic source of their being. They also began to experience a consciousness that could separate from and return to their body. This consciousness could live in multiple universes simultaneously.

The separation and return of consciousness that Mack describes reflects the experience of the mother ship and the consciousness craft. His research nudges us to ponder whether we as a species are being "pushed" into a spiritual awakening through UFO, contact encounters, as well as Near Death Experiences. Our species is not only accelerating our economic wealth, our collection of data information, our speed of travel, we are also accelerating our spiritual evolution. What once required a lifetime of disciplined, isolated, rigorous prayer, and self-denial, now was accomplished by an almost over-night NDE or close encounter. As DNA research opens human physical possibilities, our fears and limitations fade. We no longer need to limit or block our evolution; we simply need to jump into a new consciousness propelled by the power of our DNA.

Two streams—DNA and consciousness—are merging. Yet the merging is often perceived as chaotic and oppositional. Is our scientific understanding of the potential power of our DNA influencing our understanding of the enlightenment phenomenon? Or is the inflating scientific database driving our need to make sense of our human potential? Regardless of the origin, 21st Century humans seem quick to convert the image of their human body into a quantum field of potential rather than a biological machine.

Beyond our consciousness, brain, and mind, our entire body is involved in exoconsciousness. As the kundalini experience highlights, our heart energies also seem integrally involved in raising our body's frequency to manufacture a consciousness propellant. Twenty-First Century physicians are beginning to take apart the body's engine—not as mechanics, piece by piece, organ by organ, but as quantum physicians—energy by energy, frequency by frequency. The DNA phantom effect studies the quantum quality inherent in our physical bodies.

The DNA phantom effect as researched by Vladimer Poponin and ***Kirlian photography*** presents the best evidence to date of the quantum subtle energy phenomenon in our genetic makeup. In the 1990s, the Russian researcher Poponin (1998) discovered an amazing relationship between DNA and light. He developed a series of experiments to research the patterns of light in the controlled environment of a vacuum. Under the vacuum conditions the light fell into a random distribution. He then placed physical samples of DNA into the chamber and found that in the presence of genetic material, the patterns of the light particles shifted. The random pattern changed with the presence of DNA. A new pattern emerged resembling waves as they crested and fell. When DNA was withdrawn, he assumed the light would revert to the prior random distribution, but instead a new pattern emerged. The presence of DNA affected the light photons even after it was withdrawn. Did DNA possess a force that lingered long after the genetic material was withdrawn? If so, what does this say about the power of our body's presence in the physical world? The presence of our DNA seems to have a measurable effect in the physical world. If this effect can be measured, it can be understood. If it can be understood, it can be used effectively. The human heart is the starting point.

California researchers adopted the discoveries of Kilian photography and Poponin's DNA phantom effect to create a new understanding of the power of the human heart (Paddison, 1993). The **Heartmath** project sought to harness the power of the heart frequencies to accelerate and heal the body. As with kundalini experience, Heartmath researches determined that the heart possesses the most powerful electrical field in the body. This powerful field coming from the heart also has the ability to entrain or bring other energy systems in the body into its frequency. Like a mother with a fussy child, properly used, our heart pulls the disparate energy systems in our body into a higher harmony. This includes the brain. In an electrical sense, our hearts rule our heads.

In *The Hidden Power of the Heart*, HeartMath researchers also needed to incorporate the quantum model to understand the energy field of the heart (Paddison, 1993). They too turned to genetic research to understand how the powerful DNA blueprint in each and every cell of the human body holds the perfect image of the total body as a **holographic** template. Kirlian or holographic photography demonstrated a phantom effect that lingered when a leaf was cut. The Kirlian phantom leaf effect occurred when a researcher photographed a leaf with a hole cut in the center. Instead of a marred leaf, holographic photography revealed the whole, perfect leaf. Once again evidence seemed to indicate that within the DNA structure of every living thing a force remains after the genetic substance is withdrawn (Paddison, 1993, p. 167).

Is DNA a bi-product of our extraterrestrial nature? As you become familiar with our intergalactic self, the power inherent in our DNA may be used more effectively. Familiarity with your intergalactic self often stems from contact—a consciousness, physical, spiritual, and biological experience.

They were very short, shorter than five feet, and they had very large bald heads, no hair. Their heads were domed, very large. They looked like fetuses. They had no eyebrows, no eyelashes. They had very large eyes – enormous eyes – almost all brown, without much white in them. The creepiest thing about them was those eyes. Oh, man, those eyes, they just stared through me.
Travis Walton

CHAPTER 13
FENCING THE FEAR

Exoconsciousness exists on the quantum, sub-atomic level. Here, human energies interact and communicate with inter-dimensional intelligences. These intelligences manifest in the form of extraterrestrial races, orbs, angelic light beings, and mythical creatures like serpents, reptiles, and **praying mantis**. In particular, these intelligences also manifest as grays, as depicted on the cover of Whitley Strieber's book *Communion*. They may also assume familiar **humanoid** form or appear as tall ethereal shafts of light.

Research into the number of Star Visitor races varies. Colonel Corso, who wrote of seeing a dead gray in *The Day After Roswell*, spoke of 57 races. Likewise, Clifford Stone, US Army crash retrieval expert estimated 57 races. Robert Dean, formerly of the Supreme Headquarters of the Allied Powers in Europe predicts four races. Richard Boyland describes fourteen races. In *The Field Guide to Extraterrestrials*, Patrick Huyghe classifies races according to humanoid, animalian, robotic, and exotic. Michael Salla estimates 15 races, four with questionable motivations and 11 with beneficial motivations.

For now, the number of races is a secondary concern in the study of exoconsciousness. The primary issue is how we perceive, communicate, and interact with star visitors, extraterrestrials, and inter-dimensional species. Once communication has taken place, then exoconsciousness concerns itself with how we comprehend and integrate the information from these intelligent beings.

The experience of receiving information from and communication with extraterrestrial, inter-dimensional intelligences varies depending on the individual's receptivity, background, and attitude toward the experience. Individual openness, intention, and ability to remain conscious are essential. When I asked for experiences, I adopted an open, easy, reciprocal attitude toward contact.

Unlike individuals who experience abduction against their will or those who naively stumble into circumstance where they are abducted such as Travis Walton was, I simply asked and received communication and contact. Although I had vivid childhood inter-dimensional experiences, in adulthood I asked for conscious, deliberate contact. It did not happen immediately. Yet, over time, I became increasingly comfortable with the unfolding of conscious contact.

Betty and Barney Hill are a classic abduction case. While driving home late at night on a deserted New Hampshire highway they saw an object in the sky making unpredictable movements. They assumed it was either a satellite or a star. Betty described it as cigar shaped with thin shafts of colored light. As the object descended, they encountered a huge structured craft banded by a double row of windows. Barney stopped the car and got out to investigate. Inside the craft, he saw six figures wearing uniforms. He ran back to his car and began driving when he experienced a strange electronic beeping sound that vibrated the car. At that point his memory stopped.

Arriving home in the early morning hours, Barney felt an unexplained soreness at the back of his neck and the tops of his shoes were scuffed. He reported feeling unclean. Betty's sister encouraged them to examine their car for radiation. They found circles on the trunk that were highly magnetic.

Under *hypnosis*, the Hills recalled additional details. Barney recalled a "mind voice" telling him to drive deep into the woods where six men stood. They were wearing dark clothing and were backlighted with an orange glow. They both recalled being dragged out of their car, up a ramp, and into the craft. Placed on an examination table the craft staff took tissue and body fluid samples. Abducted into a craft, they experienced a harrowing physical examination they didn't understand. Were they simply specimens to be researched by extraterrestrials? Were they violated? Over time their relationship to their experience shifted from trauma to acceptance. Betty and Barney dedicated their lives to sharing their experience and gaining knowledge.

Travis Walton, whose story is featured in the movie *Fire in the Sky* is a shy, quiet man. He and his family still live in the mountains of northeast Arizona. When asked about his experience of abduction, he smiles and confesses that he stumbled into a situation where he did not belong. He stepped into a light and was sucked into a bizarre reality.

Malicious acts attributed to extraterrestrials include cattle mutilations, frightening abductions, alien craft buzzing nuclear facilities, and violating military airspace. All of these are intriguing, and invasive actions. Government and military whistleblower accounts of such overt aggressive behavior led many ufology researchers to label extraterrestrial beings as malevolent. Granted, some races seem to behave in a morally questionable manner. When attacked they defend. When observing human destructive nuclear tendencies, they defend. When humans desecrate the earth, they warn. These offensive extraterrestrial actions trigger fear, panic, and military response.

Another interpretation is that their aggressive behavior may be an ancient human relations tactic. As humans, we are acculturated by religion and society to avoid and protect ourselves from what we believe to be demonized, morally reprehensible beings. We learn at an early age to erect a fortified mental wall between perceived demonic creatures and ourselves. Is their aggressive action a purposeful means of preventing humans from contacting their race?

Another interpretation is that humans misinterpret alien actions based on human perspective. Are some extraterrestrial actions malevolent or are we simply unable to comprehend their reality and the source of their actions? Are humans unable to read the entire blueprint of life that may be available to extraterrestrial races? Thereby, are we misreading their actions? Could they possess a broader wisdom of the evolution of humans and the phases of the earth's transitions?

I have no pat answers to the issue of whether extraterrestrial beings are malevolent, protective, or benevolent. Witness accounts indicate a broad spectrum of extraterrestrial behaviors and motivations. Yet, one thing is certain. As humans, we are gradually moving into increasing awareness of extraterrestrial behaviors, motivations, perceptions, and intentions. Exoconscious communication is essential to open the dialogue regarding the intention and actions of extraterrestrials. As communication unfolds, extraterrestrial information increases. Extraterrestrial beings are yet another universe for humans to explore. The reach of the conscious universe is vast. The potential for exploration limitless.

For my part, I continue to research, listen to abductees and experiencers. Their stories are frequently peppered with fear and panic. Fear is a powerful mind control tactic. So, I choose to filter fear. I choose to research and communicate, not deny the reality and the possibility of extraterrestrials as malevolent or benevolent beings. I remain in the research stage—openly seeking wisdom.

My personal experiences with extraterrestrial beings can be characterized as gentle, awe-inspiring, and mind expanding. The beings with whom I interact are benevolent, kind, and respectful. They teach me communication techniques. They lead me to individuals and sources of knowledge. They remain respectful of my boundaries, my abilities, and my needs. They remain respectful that I am a human being, albeit with a legacy from other dimensions.

Initially, as an adult, extraterrestrials began communicating with me telepathically. The experience was very similar to communicating as a medium with souls who have passed over. They sent thought forms and visions that I deciphered. They identified themselves and communicated their message. Then, they waited for my response. Frequently the telepathic communication was brief, it seemed as though they could not sustain the earth frequency. These communications lasted for a brief moment, then their form changed or they dissolved. Looking back, perhaps it was my awkward first steps at communication that required extraterrestrials to send dense, easy to read packets of information. They placed the easy reader in my mind, and then departed while I deciphered the meaning. My mind slowly fingered the symbols and images. Like a child learning to read, I gradually sounded out, formed the symbols ecstatic when I learned a new message.

Exoconscious Communication Comes Online

My communication abilities evolved through distinct phases. I am a natural shaman, able to travel through dimensions, bringing back information for others and myself. For many years, I performed as a shaman without labeling my abilities. It felt natural, even effortless. I would be "called." My response assumed that I would travel wherever I was needed and work with whomever was present. My shamanic phase began in childhood and continues today.

During the second phase, orbs, intelligent balls of light, began to appear during the early evening hours in my home. They would gather in my living room, communicate, or simply glow, announcing their presence. During this phase I developed a confident, calm relationship with intelligent orbs. Today, they continue to live, move, and communicate with me. They are as real as the television signal in my home. They are a different form of information and energy.

Next, the orbs began congregating at night in my bedroom. They would waken me from sleep, a gathering of energy in the corner of my room. Awakened, they would literally whiz, squealing over my head, communicating, and pulsing. I sensed they were unable to hold physical form in our earth dimension. They needed to move, dart, communicate, and depart quickly. There was no need for me to "hold" their energy—they manifested as a fleeting intelligence. It was up to me to remain conscious and communicate.

After the orbs, a "night school" phase began. It was intense and earnest. I was awakened at night as the ceiling of my bedroom came alive. It appeared similar to a multi-dimensional crystal screen. I could mentally touch the screen ceiling and it would come alive. It literally communicated. Symbols and forms appeared, punched down from above. It was my response-ability to integrate the symbols and remember the meaning. Slowly my eyes and my mind traced the forms, as wisdom opened. Night after night, my alphabet increased. I could read the symbols and shapes. My vocabulary matured. My communication skills improved markedly. This night school phase lasted perhaps a year or more. Class was not in-session every night. There were deliberate breaks designed to allow for integration of the information.

As extraterrestrial disclosure accelerates through our culture, it provides a deeper understanding of symbols and forms as a communication vehicle. And I mean vehicle. Symbols and forms possess power and limitless potential. Symbols and forms, as energized forms of information, can transform into living, operational technology. Symbols and forms come alive, breathe, and then begin to move, communicate, and operate.

The ability of symbols to come alive and be operational holds important, perhaps revolutionary, significance for world religions that have preserved and defined much of the symbolic vocabulary of our human race. Symbols saturate our belief systems. In religion, symbols can hold us in place, secure and protected. Through exoconsciousness, symbols can fertilize potent powerful questions that can propel us into our future. In technology, symbols can be used to create a designated, engineered, and operational entity.

So how does this happen? How do symbols come alive? How do symbols transform into technology?

During 2007, citizens in California sent researcher Linda Moulton Howe testimony and photos of drone vehicles that were materializing then disappearing. To me, these drones looked like flying birdcages. Some photos showed distinct symbols carved into the underside of the crafts. After many months of speculation, a rather controversial witness, Isaac, came forward. Many experts questioned Isaac's testimony due to his writing style, description of security protocol, and willingness to release confidential information. However questionable, some of his information provided important insights.

Isaac claimed to have worked in a hybrid military, government, and corporate research program named CARET from 1984 to 1987. CARET stood for "Commercial Applications Research for Extra-terrestrial Technology." It focused on anti-gravity propulsion systems research. He asserted that extraterrestrial technology was different from human technology. Unlike human technology, extraterrestrial technology was not dependent on the integration of computer software, or programming, that required hardware in order to run. In other words, no matter how effectively humans compose computer programming, it needs hardware to implement its function. In comparison, during the extraterrestrial technology process, software becomes its own hardware. Symbols, as software, become hardware.

On her Earthfiles website, Linda Moulton Howe provided a forum for Isaac's testimony. It is also available at the website, http://isaaccaret.fortunecity.com/. Isaac claimed that during extraterrestrial-based research and development, symbols or forms came alive. The symbols, forms, or patterns birthed extraterrestrial vehicles and their accompanying propulsion systems. Software birthed hardware. The implications for consciousness are vast!

Here is how Isaac explained the process:

> But their technology is different. It really did operate like the magical piece of paper sitting on a table, in a manner of speaking. They had something akin to a language, which could quite literally execute itself, at least in the presence of a very specific type of field. The language, a term I am still using very loosely, is a system of symbols (which does admittedly very much resemble a written language) along with geometric forms and patterns that fit together to form diagrams that are themselves functional. Once they are drawn, so to speak, on a suitable surface made of a suitable material and in the presence of a certain type of field, they immediately begin performing the desired tasks. It really did seem like magic to us, even after we began to understand the principles behind it (Howe).

Though experts remain skeptical of Isaac's testimony, he provided an essential framework for visualizing what may be our next step in technology as we move out of the hardware, software dialectic into an integrated method of technological creation via symbols that come alive.

Are scientists and engineers already using these extraterrestrial type transformations from symbol, form, and pattern into technology? Possibly, if not probably. As our human race catapults into an almost unimaginable future, a magical reality opens. Drones appear and disappear. Witnesses come forward with startling testimony. Experiencers share night school curriculums of symbols and forms. The timing is perfect. Extraterrestrial information is communicated through many sources. All can participate. Each individual chooses.

On the Download

Another phase of communication commenced as my communication level heightened. When night school was over, my primary communication technique became downloads. For years I have received information downloads. Downloads are pulsating, quick generations of information—bits, bites, of energy that seem to move into my being, usually through the top of my head, or occasionally it showers my body. It feels like computer code that enters my body and saturates my being. Intuitively, it seems to integrate energy forms into my physical body (DNA, cells) as well as my mental and spiritual body. It is a holistic experience. The extraterrestrials do not call these experiences a download; that is my term. It feels as though I am being programmed and downloaded, similar to a computer. Downloads are simply a form of communication. I am engineered to receive, retrieve, and transmit information.

As I continued experiencing downloads, they intensified. As they intensified, the protocol changed. The extraterrestrial race might manifest and identify itself. Instead of automatically having a twinge, a quick feeling of a download, I would receive a telepathic message that a download was coming. At this point I can choose to accept, reject, or delay the transmission. I usually accept. The telepathic messages alerting me to a download may come in the early morning as I am doing yoga or meditating, during a quiet break in my day, when I am watching TV, or occasionally when I awakened during the night. I am instructed to lie still as the code enters. I am usually alerted if the transmission will be lengthy. At the completion of the transmission I am told that I can move.

I am unsure of the purpose of downloads, but I can speculate. Since receiving downloads my telepathic and psychic abilities heightened. My intellectual abilities refined and strengthened. My mind grasps complex ideas with enhanced ease. My physical body feels as though it is realigning and filling with light. Perhaps my DNA is being awakened and transformed. My ability to communicate inter-dimensionally and inter-species accelerates. Downloads redefine my human nature. My extraterrestrial legacy awakens to my conscious mind with each download.

Occasionally prior to working with clients, I receive a download. Then as our session progresses I become conscious of the extraterrestrial presence that brought me the download. Together we work as a team during the session. I am able to visualize the extraterrestrial's energy and movements around the client. They do not abruptly enter the session, but ask permission to join. Clients have differing extraterrestrial makeup, so different races appear as we work together. Blue Andromedian beings manifest for some, reptilian beings for others, and tall shafts of ethereal light beings for others.

Downloads are a direct result of my willingness to work with various extraterrestrial races and transmit their communication. Downloads prepare me to receive specific energetic forms of information. Each extraterrestrial race has a unique frequency expressed as symbols and language. Downloads create channels in my consciousness for the transmissions of various extraterrestrial races. We work together. I agree to become a conscious channel and grant permission for the gateway channel to be formed. Once the channel is in place the energetic information moves back and forth between the extraterrestrial race and me. Like learning a new skill or language, downloads involve and infiltrate my entire being—my brain, mind, body, and spirit.

Is it unusual that I receive communication and downloads from extraterrestrials? Or are all humans intimately connected to star beings, through our DNA, our bloodline? Yes, it is a strong possibility. I now perceive humans through new eyes. I see their inter-dimensional being. Some individuals have obvious star lineages and appear as human replicas of various grays, or humanoids, reptiles. We possess legacies from other dimensions. Once an individual experiences a star legacy, it remains their choice to participate, accept, or reject.

Simultaneous with downloads, I experienced a healthy release of thought forms I no longer needed. Like armor, I removed many thought forms, perceived authorities, belief, and attitudes. Layer after layer dissolved. Sure, the removal of certain thought forms, beliefs, and authorities left some tender places that needed to heal. Tapping into your extraterrestrial lineage requires patience, self-nurturing, and compassion. Some layers required years of work to remove, release, and resolve. Some layers seemed limitless and complex, these required assistance from a group of alternative healers. Removal of these layers required acceptance that they would eventually dissolve. Acceptance and intention were essential to the process. Patience, self-care, and self-love provided the healing salve. When the unwanted thought forms finally dissolves, you feel free and happy.

As a result of release from unwanted thought forms, an increase in psychic ability, and continuing downloads, I am in touch with my extraterrestrial being, my source from the stars. Am I a hybrid? Perhaps. Perhaps all humans are hybrids. We are star beings mixed with the clay of human nature.

So what is your hybrid mix? Richard Boylan developed a questionnaire (see Appendix) to help identify star being tendencies. It is a quantitative matrix and as such provides a framework for considering who you are in comparison with others. No two individuals are the same. Don't take your numbers too seriously. We all experience varying levels of consciousness that is affected by our level of stress, self-acceptance, and background. A high psychic friend became upset during a conference hosted at her home. During a fun experiment, her psychic ability measured low. Fretting to me, I explained that as hostess to over 50 people in her home, she was certainly under stress and her mind was far from relaxed. Environments change. Stress levels change. Beliefs change.

I found it interesting to answer the questionnaire, review my answers, and then set it aside. In time, additional abilities unfolded and my scores changed. At different times in our life we are conscious of different abilities. See who you are now. See who you are at a later time.

Sirius is a winterbluegreen star.
Robert Francis, "Blue Winter"

CHAPTER 14
COUNCIL COMMUNICATION

Extraterrestrial contact has a natural progression. Initially, my contact came via individual entities—grays, humanoids, blue beings, mantis-like creatures, and angelic-like presences. Each appeared, eager to communicate. Often whizzing orbs awakened me. They prepared me for a later visitation by the vast black wrapped eyes of extraterrestrial beings.

Prior to downloads, for years I attended a night school where I gained knowledge through symbols that were literally pressed through my bedroom ceiling—not unlike a crop circle formation in reverse. The experience was reminiscent of ancient cultures such as Egypt where individuals lay in halls blanketed by symbols. On an unconscious level I intuited the meaning of the symbols. Symbols pressed through my ceiling awakened my memory and shifted my consciousness. I removed the blindfold of my earth beliefs and language systems to recover knowledge. Often symbols were accompanied by visitations from extraterrestrial beings accompanied by Egyptian personalities such as Sekmet, Hathor, Thoth, Isis, and Osirius. Blended into Egyptian were Biblical personalities—Mother Mary, Magdalene, the family of Jesus, James, Joseph, Ezekiel, Ezra, Enoch, Abraham.

Announcement of a pending extraterrestrial visitation also came through animals—coyote, owl, lizard. One evening while leaving a fast food restaurant I saw a magnificent owl perched on a tall parking lot light pole. The owl simply stared at me. I understood the message—contact would come that evening. Extraterrestrials often use a screen technique to calm humans. They employ familiar animals and beings as a screen hiding their presence to prohibit fear and panic. Experiencers relate being on ET craft surrounded by a cast of familiar and unfamiliar characters—a huge reptilitan being next to a human-like female dressed like a nurse. A small gray next to a familiar Star Trek commander. A Native American next to a snake being. Often experiencers initially recall screened memories of extraterrestrial contact as a large owl, or an angel, or a Native American. Other times they recall an eye or a slender finger. As humans calm, they allow the contact to progress. In my experience, contact progressed from individual, to small groups to large councils.

Like humans, extraterrestrials travel in groups. They identify themselves as assemblies or councils and may attach a number to their identity. I am privileged to work with two councils, the Council of Nine and the Council of Twelve. Each council brings different information, communicates in a unique manner, and seems to reside in a different dimension. Perhaps the Council of Twelve resides in the twelfth dimension and the Council of Nine in the ninth dimension. Twelve and nine are powerful numbers, regardless of where they reside. The time and date of my birth is a mixture of the numbers 6,9,12, and 24. I came into this earth life stamped with dimensional identities.

When I first experienced the Council of Twelve, I didn't ask to communicate with them, they simply appeared. They felt familiar, as though I communicated with them in a past life or in another dimension. As with previous extraterrestrial experiences, the council was respectful and kind. Often they came as an entire council group. They gathered around a large geometric shape where I was also seated. Other times, individuals from the group appeared separately. I immediately sensed they came from the Twelve.

The Council of Twelve is a United Nations type gathering of many races. In my experience, the council is composed of star beings from Orion, Arcturus, Andromeda, Sirius, Lyra, Pleiades, Grays, Alpha Centauri, Tau Ceti, Annunaki, as well as Reptilian, Serpent, and bird-like beings.

Initially, when the Council of Twelve manifested I would simply receive communications. They communicated telepathically and were easily understood. Then with time our conversations became more like a dialogue—a give and take of ideas, requests, and information. During the initial phases of our work together, I seemed to lie within the group, as if in a meditative state, while they communicated. Then as our communication continued, it became more interactive. Increasingly they revealed their presence. Their dimension feels structured, somewhat linear and geometric. Not unlike our earth plane, yet different. Some beings were fluid illumination and ethereal; others were definable creatures and humanoids.

With time, I became one with them. I suppose counting me as a human visitor, there was a total of 13 present. 13 is another powerful, magical number. At times I questioned whether I was a visitor. Intuitively, I felt a deep connection to the Twelve, as though we were one. If so, I am connected to them in my human form. I believe many experiencers and contactees have similar feelings. I believe all humans have a connection to inter-dimensional councils or assemblies. How else can we explain our allegiance to earth life and yet our ability to communicate dimensionally? At some point one's consciousness needs to explore anomalous experience. Our consciousness strives to make sense of off-worlds that feel comfortable and safe, yet distant and strange.

To communicate the experience of the Twelve, I sought biblical and mythological paradigms. I needed to give the experience a conscious structure. With my background, I turned to spiritual, mythological, and religious language. Perhaps I had been "sent" by the council. Perhaps I "represented" the council, was "one" with the council, or possessed a "cord" to the council. Whatever the connection, I "belonged" to the community of the council.

Of course the next step of spiritual, mythological, and religious language plunges one into deep water, or as it were, deep space. There one begins to speak of "having a divine right," of "being chosen," of acting as a self-designated "ambassador," even a "messiah."

I simply chose to not take that leap. I shied away from that storyline. It was fraught with ancient potholes. I was simply communicating and connected to the Council of Twelve, which was as far as my ego was permitted to go. Beyond laid pitfalls and dangerous territory. As I kept it simple, my communication and confidence level flourished. I refused to complicate the alliance.

Historically, spiritual alliances gather as a dozen: Jesus Christ and the 12 disciples, 12 signs of the Zodiac, Rosicrucians directed by Councils of 12, and New Age channelers of 12.

In my experience, the Twelve represented an assembly of alien races who formed a cooperative alliance. They eagerly communicated with me and opened doors of knowledge regarding physics, biology, healing, and mental powers, along with inter-dimensional travel. Often they stirred me from a sound sleep to send a clear communication. Telepathically clear communications eventually unfolded in my conscious mind. They assisted with opening human possibilities, reframing old beliefs. For example, working with them I called into question mainstream thought forms regarding health, the human body, and aging. With their assistance, I easily removed, released, and resolved thought forms I no longer needed. With their assistance, I easily connected with individuals and groups with similar perspectives.

Living and relating with the Council of Twelve has opened my life to an astounding, limitless abundance of resources and knowledge. While I often received specific information, my primary experience was of a subtle, intuitive nature. Seemingly over-night my attitudes and thoughts transformed. Today, I acknowledge mainstream scientific, historical, and religious thinking, yet live in a broader expanse of knowledge. I did not experience a war of knowledge or run a race to prove fact or reality. Through the council, I simply received and integrated an intuitive knowing that expanded my beliefs, attitudes, and knowledge. Information realities resided side by side, harmoniously shifting facts and data to fit the dimension.

Interesting how our government formed a committee of scientists, military, and government personnel, called *Majestic 12*, or *MJ12* to investigate UFO activity after the Roswell crash. This committee has been the source of much debate and research in the field of ufology and exopolitics. December 1984, filmmaker Jaime Shandera received an unmarked package in the mail containing a roll of undeveloped film. Shandera and his colleague, UFO investigator William Moore, developed the film. The film held copies of what looked like secret briefing papers for then President–elect Dwight Eisenhower dated 11-18-52. The files indicated that Truman established MJ12 to investigate the growing number of alien craft sightings. Within ufology circles, MJ12 has been dissected, debunked, and investigated with various conclusions. Ryan Wood's book *Majic Eyes Only:Earth's Encounters with Extraterrestial Technology,* provides a scholarly overview of our government's role in UFO sightings, crash retrieval, and extraterrestrials.

Were the members of MJ12 communicating with the same council? Probably. As they say…numbers don't lie. The nature of the council is open and receptive to contact. They are intimately connected to the affairs of planet earth. Yet, one need not be a government official, military officer, or world leader to gain access. The Council of Twelve potentially cords to each citizen of earth.

Working with the Twelve, I shifted prior religious beliefs concerning competing dualistic ideas such as heaven and hell, divine and devil. For example, I now view the classic image of burning in hell as a positive illustration of the cleansing energies of fire. Fire energies promote an immediate, accelerated burn of all we no longer need—worn out beliefs, attachments, and behaviors. Ask anyone who moved to Phoenix about fire energies they experienced. Once you give them a chance to ponder the question, they will begin to tell you of the rapid changes that moved through their lives as a result of their move to the Sonoran Desert. New arrivals may not consciously intend to burn, but day after day, people arrive from across the nation and the world to settle into the Phoenix fire energies to do their work. The end result of the fire energies moves an individual into a position of polarity, a centered place of energy flow where duality no longer pulls.

The pioneer of polarity, Dr. Randolph Stone, asserted that the underlying atomic and magnetic structure of the body possessed properties of attraction and repulsion. To achieve the desirable state of polarity or health through an easy energy flow, he developed techniques for the removal of energy blocks, which he considered the cause of pain and disease in the body. Removal of energy blocks permitted the body to realign into a seamless energy field. Fire energies can melt blocks and move an individual beyond duality into polarity. In this light, hell might be our salvation on earth—a means to reach the polarity of peace.

While working with the Twelve, a Council of Nine appeared. There was an ease with the Council of Nine, because by the time they appeared, I was proficiently communicating with the Twelve. In comparison, the Council of Nine felt dense and focused. They were more agenda oriented.

Unlike the Council of Twelve, I discovered that the Council of Nine has a lengthy recorded history. Esoterically oriented individuals have written about their experience with the Council of Nine. Lynn Picknett and Clive Prince thoroughly examined the history of the Council of Nine in their book *The Stargate Conspiracy: Revealing the Truth Behind Extraterrestrial Contact, Military Intelligence and the Mysteries of Ancient Egypt.* This book is a "must read" for experiencers who want to link their contact to historical and political personalities and movements.

Picknett and Prince researched the Council of Nine thread as it originated in ancient cultures such as Atlantis and then moved into Sumeria, Egypt, Central and South America. According to them, Schwaller de Lubicz's three volume *The Temple of Man* posits that the number 9 is of major importance in the Pythagorean system. They also correlated the Council of Nine with the Mars-Egypt connection detailed by Richard Hoagland (Enterprise Mission website) and James Hurtak (*Keys of Enoch*). Their research solidified the importance of the innate extraterrestrial—Sumerian—Egyptian connection I felt since early childhood. Was I birthed with this cord open and operative? If so, are all humans connected, yet not aware? The further I ventured into open communication with the councils, the stronger my feeling that this cord to extraterrestrial and ancient cultures defines who we are, where we came from, what we are to do on earth, and where we are evolving as a race of beings.

According to Picknett and Prince, connection to the Council of Nine defined our political and religious history. "We gradually uncovered evidence of the extraordinary hold that these alleged non-human intelligences have over top industrialists, cutting edge scientists, popular entertainers, radical parapsychologists, and key figures in military and intelligence circles. We were to find that the Nine's influence even extends to the threshold of the White House itself" (162). Their work uncovered the extraterrestrial roots of mind control research, New Age religion, Star Trek type films, and paranormal personalities. In many of these arenas, research was not always complimentary and frequently focused on a conspiratorial agenda.

Picknett and Prince identify several agendas that may define the work of the Nine. A powerful cabal may be training individuals to communicate with the Nine in an effort to obtain important information for their own ends. Others in contact with the Nine may be deliberately misleading the populace that "contact is imminent." Or it may be a combination of both, where contact with the Nine is made in conjunction with cultural and media efforts to prepare the population for contact. Or finally, those making contact may simply be duped by the Nine, who may be a deliberate fabrication by a covert power.

The Nine remains a mystery. Any or all of these motivations may be operative. Each person develops their path into extra-dimensional realities. It unfolds gradually, one bread crumb at a time. As I learned in **Neural Linguistic Programming**, the meaning of the communication is the response you get. Content of communication is seven percent. Context, process and structure are 93 percent. And so it goes with extraterrestrial and extra-dimensional contact—over time with orb phenomenon, symbols, voices, beings, and councils—the context and structure of my life shifted in a deliberate process. Who I became as a result of the experience was more significant than what was "said" or "communicated."

Was I given significant messages by these councils? Yes, but not always. I was repeatedly warned of the tenuous state of planet earth and their concern for human welfare. They communicated that the vibration of earth was not hospitable for prolonged visitation. Messages were relayed concerning bombings and terrorism as well as political infighting. Several times they notified me of an incoming visitation that paralleled increased craft sightings.

Before 911, messages increased. Prior to 911, I had a vivid dream of a "water tower" with the initials WT. In my dream, the water tower was on fire and humans were leaping off. During the day strong messages mounted. I was told that many would die. It was a fearful communication. For days I felt like I was on "high alert." As the morning of 911 dawned, a radio broadcast awakened me with the news coverage. I lay in my bed and visualized the reality of the terror that had been communicated, then I inhaled an energy of peace and light. I had no idea of how many were departing the earth plane during that tragedy. I sensed there were many. So I calmly moved my spirit to theirs. Together we shifted out of the fire, turmoil, and terror into peace, calm, and light. My spirit moved easily from one to another—men, women, children. I dressed for work, drove down the Beeline, and remained in my office most of the day, holding a space of light, love, and peace. Looking back, the communications prior to 911 were not meant to frighten me; they were intended to prepare me. They prepared me to relax amid the terror and become peace.

I tucked these communiqués into my heart and proceeded with my life. Living in the UFO community, I learned quickly the hazards of making rash announcements based on extraterrestrial communications. Rash announcements and end of time pronouncements trigger fear and block possibilities for change and peace. Early on, I adopted a quiet mode. If asked, I answered. When it was time to write, I did. Otherwise I maintained a low profile, concentrating on the amazing personal transformations and paths to knowledge opened by extraterrestrial contact.

I now maintain contact with confidence, strengthened by the experience that there are many dimensions and many intelligences. Like Jesus described, our reality has many mansions, many rooms. At one point during a hypnosis session I visualized myself as a central being with numerous cords branching off my body into openings or portals. With that image, I understood myself as a multi-dimensional being granted access to many mansions, many worlds. I possess a passport, as do each and every one of us. With experience I understood that each dimension communicates differently with a distinct style and vibration. As humans it is our response-ability to discriminate these realities, opening to communicate, yet maintaining our earth life. Fear, terror, panic, and anxiety effectively shut down our channels of communication. In fearful circumstances we only concentrate on the dimension broadcasting fear. Television networks and major media outlets successfully use this technique.

When dealing with fear and terror via extraterrestrial dimensions, you simply need to stay heart-centered, calm, and peaceful. Fearful predictions are simply one of many styles of dimensional communication. There is no need for a major announcement or the creation of a new religion, guru, or political movement. Extraterrestrial contact simply beckons you to become who you are—an intelligent, multi-dimensional being—fine tuned and capable of transforming incoming threats and apocalyptic times into peaceful co-existence and polarity.

All that remained was that familiar indefinable lump in the chest. It had nothing to do with problems or perplexities. It did not seem specifically related to anything. It was simply the going-away lump, that had been there when I was a child and was as uncontrollable now as then. Leaving the seaside after the summer was over; leaving home for the seaside; leaving houses, country and city, casual and important, temporary and permanent - any place that you had made with difficulty and affection your home. In fact, simply going away.

Why, I sometimes argued with myself, you might be your great-great-grandmother, who never left her New England house or village, instead of someone who traveled constantly. What did they call it in New England when they felt this same thing, this lump in the throat, this sick feeling in the pit of the stomach, when the trunks were strapped up and the hat boxes were piled high at the front door, waiting for the carriage? "Journey-proud," they said. "She's just journey-proud."

Anne Morrow Lindbergh, *Listen! The Wind*

CHAPTER 15
JOURNEY-PROUD

Exoconsciousness operates as mother ship and craft. Jaimie Maussan, a Mexican newscaster, collected videos of a mother ship expelling and receiving craft. Through spiritual work and visualization, I experienced bodily knowledge that I too was a mother craft, expelling and receiving my conscious body. I possessed the ability to travel and return home. Hawaiians tell of the power of the Goddess Pele, who resides in the volcano on the Big Island. She is loving, powerful, and destructive. Legends tell that when Pele feels it is time for you to come to the Islands, she inhales you. Then when it is time for you to leave, she spits you out. Perhaps exhale is a gentler metaphor than spit. When Pele exhales, you simply go home. Yet also, when you experience her inhale to the islands, you are home.

Islanders love framing their comings and goings in the Pele story. One woman lived on the islands until energy and money drained. Then Pele exhaled her to another island—Tahiti—where she married and started a business. Years later Pele inhaled her again and she returned to the islands, divorced, and ready to complete her education and buy land to settle. I wonder—who creates the inhale and exhale? Pele or the traveler? Or do the two forces simply cooperate to arrive at a destination then depart?

Similarities with extraterrestrial energies are striking. When it was time for me to know inter-dimensional intelligences, extraterrestrials, and councils—they inhaled me. I was sucked into their vortex of energy. Once there, I decided, like traveling to Hawaii, I loved their energy and reality. I could travel to the "mainland" and maintain my earth life and also easily return to their reality. Now, I bi-locate with ease. I belong in both worlds.

As I delve into inter-dimensional and extraterrestrial reality I find my earth life also deepens and expands. It is as though the interconnected system of dimensions enhance one another. As an earth being, my sensory abilities are heightened, my emotions fuller and lighter, my physical body healthier. As I step back to examine who I am and where I have been, I see no liabilities. The journey is wonderful, the benefits far beyond my imagination. Today I am a citizen of many dimensions.

And, the fun is that I continue to learn. Learning and knowledge are limitless. A primary focus of my learning continues to be consciousness and understanding the changes, transformations, abilities I experience. Books, fellow experiencers and researchers continue to bring information.

Colonel Corso, the co-author of *The Day After Roswell*, worked with inter-dimensional information, which he termed the "nut file." Corso was responsible for the artifacts of the Roswell crash housed in his file cabinet at the Pentagon. Under the Army's authority, he systematically parceled items from the Roswell crash to research corporations, military contractors, and select military installations. Corso would initially meet with an individual responsible for research that might further the Army's understanding of alien craft and alien biology. Then, as Corso departed the meeting, so would any trace of their conversation. The artifact would simply be integrated into on-going research and the sources disappear over time.

Corso wrote of Dayton's Wright Patterson's research into the consciousness interface between alien and craft. Biologically and psychically, the alien guided and maneuvered the craft. Alien and the craft were one. Body, mind, and craft were one. As in the Jaimie Massaun video, the craft seemed conscious. Was this conscious craft a futuristic example of *singularity*, where technological advancements such as artificial intelligence leaps beyond human abilities and creates a new world? In this new world humans no longer compete with technology. The competition is over. Technology triumphs human ability. Did the Roswell crash artifacts provide Corso with the vision of humans engineered with artificial intelligence? Is the alien-craft interface an example of futuristic bionic humans who cooperate with a conscious craft?

Both futuristic scenarios are fast becoming our reality. Were these alien beings from the crash site representative of our future? If so who are we becoming?

According to Corso, the alien's brain was quickly researched then autopsied with the best equipment and knowledge available in 1947. While the report indicated similarities between the human and the alien brain, there were striking differences. The medical examiner reported that readings taken from the alien's brain, prior to death, indicated long-low frequency waves. "And the examiner referred to a description by one of the Roswell Army Air Field doctors that the creature's brain lobes seem to have been not just physiologically and neurologically integrated but integrated by an electromagnetic current as well" (Corso, p. 210).

The essential research component of space travel may be the human brain and the power of the conscious and unconscious mind. While NASA preoccupies our imagination with rockets blasting into orbit, space stations, and planet exploration, are we missing an essential ingredient? Nuts and bolts rocket science is essential, yet research into the human brain and consciousness provide clues to the navigation system. As a space faring race, we require a radical orientation, a shift from human consciousness to exoconsciousness.

Corso relates how the Soviets in the late 50s were using psychics to practice kinetic mind control. Our government turned to famed psychics like Uri Geller and Plutarch to do similar research. Both governments realized that consciousness held the key to space travel. They both acknowledged aliens used their brain waves to navigate the craft. It was rumored that the aliens wore a headband that transferred their consciousness to the craft. They were part of the integrated circuit of the craft.

Within consciousness, the power of long-low frequency waves was essential. And so we witnessed the advent of Silva Mind Control, Transcendental Meditation, and Eslan. These mind movements raced to unlock the secrets within human consciousness. These mind movements were technologically monitored, with a strong scientific (Scientology?) basis.

While world religions possessed an ancient heritage of meditation, prayer, centering, whirling, and yoga, the government wanted to harness this long-low wave frequency for space travel, so they birthed their own

"New Age" groups. And they met with success. Twenty-first century humans are rapidly becoming acculturated to ancient consciousness arts. The consciousness disciplines we choose to practice are modifying our brains and our conscious abilities

One of my favorite mythologists, Will Henry, shows a video of Egyptian Sufis performing a whirling dervish. They spin until their bodies literally transform into disc shaped craft. What is happening in their consciousness? How are they harnessing their brain waves to transform their physical being?

As the future unfolds, questions swirl regarding human participation in technological advancement and space travel. Are humans relegated behind security lines, travelers in the airport without a boarding pass? Or are the intellectual and security blocks illusions? I believe exoconsciousness and ufology provide a participatory experience of the unfolding future. They provide an experience that dissolves fear and generates creative solutions for the human race and our planet earth.

Exoconscious Solution

For decades, ufologists have released information from experiencers, whistle-blowers, and witnesses concerning possible destructive technological scenarios in our earth's future. Exopolitics focused the ufologists' warnings with political/historical documents and witness testimony. Exposing extraterrestrial influences on our technological advancement, they offer a political perspective replete with warnings and workable solutions. Exoconsciousness, cooperating with the foundational work of ufologists and exopolitics, provides the consciousness component. Framing consciousness within an extraterrestrial, cosmic context invites creative perspectives of human abilities. Exoconsciousness offers workable solutions that stem from cosmic-based inner- and extra-dimensional consciousness functioning beyond the bounds of space and time.

The effectiveness of an exoconsciousness approach relies heavily on the ufologists' research and the continued strength of the exopolitics political perspective. As information regarding our extraterrestrial lineage and inter-dimensional universe emerges, it will be filtered through the respective ufology, exopolitics, and exoconsciousness lens. Cooperatively, conclusions essential to the survival of our human species as inter-planetary beings will be found.

Viewing the future with prophetic eyes, consciousness research illuminating human exoconscious abilities comes none too soon. The threats of singularity, electromagnetic pollution, mind control, and non-lethal weaponry call for a response.

Intelligent machines assert the right to exist among humans. Mind and matter compete for the same dwelling place. Can Earth's environment accommodate both? If the levels of electronic pulse contamination are any indication, Earth appears to struggle. Machines seem to be occupying the superior advantage, with researchers eager to birth the next generation for humans to consume. Electronic, nuclear, and alternative fuel systems necessary to power intelligent machines pollute the human environment in a silent, sickly assault. Our consumption may either lead to destruction or re-creation.

According to Robert Becker in *The Body Electric: Electromagnetism and the Foundation of Life* (1984), invisible forces of ***electromagnetism*** are rapidly deteriorating the human central nervous system. Stress response heightens and short-term memory falters. Resultant hyperactivity and disturbed sleep patterns affect daily routine. In April 2005, Dr. Jill Meara, the British Deputy Director of the Health Protection Agency, publicly acknowledged the reality of electromagnetic allergies. She advised sufferers to keep their distance from electronic devices and to purchase alternative low-power appliances.

We swim in an ever-increasing electrical current, compromising our immune system and spawning virulent viruses. Spend thirty minutes in a 50-something gym and listen to the litany of diseases plaguing the electrical body—Lupus, Fibromyalgia, Lyme disease. These diseases may not be new, but they have become all too familiar to an exponentially increasing number of humans.

Are machines making us sick? Are galactic storms affecting our inner compass and psychic ability? Are stealth silent weapons from an invisible enemy assaulting us? The answer appears affirmative. For many, an immediate reaction to this knowledge is fear. Fear that darkens the vision of possibilities. During fear, humans are blind to the secret mirror image that seems to have been placed in human nature. This mirror image may hold our second chance.

An exoconscious species, we travel this earth life aware of multiple realities, whether conscious or unconscious. A cosmic collective unconscious memory stores past world glimpses of destructive technological advancements, earth devastation, and insidious weaponry assaults. Many are working to bring these memories forward, out of the cave, and into the light. As a community of humans, we need to bring the memory forth gradually, allowing our conscious mind to adjust to the past trauma and sorrow. Releasing ancient fears, we hold ourselves in compassion, accountable for our action and our fears. Releasing ancient fears, we hold ourselves in faith, accountable for our power and our possibilities. The reality of our memory of devastation, destruction, and attack is balanced by the reality of the second chance, hard-wired into our bodies and evolutionary paths that humans enjoy.

Maureen Dowd is the most recent author heralding the demise of the male Y chromosome in her book *Are Men Necessary?* (2005). As women gain power, is the Y chromosome doomed to disappear? Some geneticists concur. The X and Y chromosomes that started out with the same amount of about 1,000 genes are facing separate fates. While X remains vital, Y now has less than 80 genes.

What does the future hold for our dualistic genetic heritage that spawned love songs and beautiful children? David Page of MIT on a National Public Radio program offers hope. He points to the second chance that seems to be hard-wired into our chromosomes. "The Y chromosome has been secretly creating backup copies of its most important genes. These are stored in the DNA as mirror images or palindromes—which read the same way forwards and backwards. (Madam, I'm Adam is a famous example.)"

Our bodies seem to be hard-wired to weather genetic transformations. What of our consciousness? How will we move through the assaults from electromagnetic pollution, galactic storms, and mind weaponry? Is there a second chance?

The ancient homeopathic remedy, "like cures like" holds promise as a solution for electromagnetic pollution. Lance Wilson, an independent researcher, in his article "Can we Stop Cancer from Frequency Pollution," proposes that "by sending in ELF—Extremely Low Frequencies—into an area of known and above average cancer rates in the middle of the night as people sleep, you could boost their immune system and help keep free radicals in their body at bay." He proposes that our immune system strengthens with the 8.5 to 7.89 Hz frequencies, the range of Mother Earth's lullaby known as the **Schumann Resonance**. Could the answer to our allergic reaction to electronic pollution, such as power lines and cell phones, be simpler than to slumber to the heartbeat of Mother Earth and awaken re-armored to face the day?

Cosmic super waves and solar eruptions present a more formidable threat. Past-life pictures of medieval throngs fleeing incoming cosmic chaos flash through our memory. Do we simply stand and face our possible demise or are there alternative memories we might access? Perhaps our memory of the underworld needs to be revisited?

Levenda's *Sinister Forces—the Nine: A Grimoire of American Political Witchcraft* (2005) points to the primeval vortices that permitted entry into the underworld—the physical and psychic points of entry. While the occult and religion have functioned as gatekeepers to this underworld, it is time for them to relinquish their grip. They may not yet be ready, but the time is near. The curtain will be pulled from the nightmare underworld scenarios. The beauty beneath will be recognized. In the event of cosmic super waves, asteroids, and nuclear winter, humans may need to once more move safely underground. Aligned with the heart of the earth, we as a civilization may need to move down and bundle safe against the storms above. Exoconscious memory grants intuitive access to the points of entry and the safe passage below.

Military non-lethal assault weapons and mind-control technologies present an immediate threat with political and consciousness implications. Investigative researchers have exposed the patents and applications of these most lethal, ironically termed "non-lethal" weapons. Is there a viable mirror image, a second chance against an attack by this next generation of weaponry? As the question appears, the answer emerges. The words Mary and army are composed of the same letters. According to the Kabala, each letter holds a message for those who seek an answer.

The Miriam Mother archetype points to the human potential of intuition and knowing. It is another potential that our cultural gatekeepers are reluctantly relinquishing. The mainstream tipping point was reached when Malcolm Gladwell's *Blink: the Power of Thinking without Thinking* (2005) perched atop the bestseller list, presenting scientific validation of our intuition. Gladwell terms it our "adaptive unconscious," which he distinguishes from our Freudian unconscious. "This new notion of the adaptive unconscious is thought of, instead, as a kind of giant computer that quickly and quietly processes a lot of the data we need in order to keep functioning as human beings." This ability functions in a microsecond as innate knowing.

Whether rooted in the mud of the Mother (M theory) or our neural circuitry, our adaptive unconscious may be a first-line defense against assault. One of the more malevolent aspects of mind-control weaponry is the tendency for humans to become entranced and simply to bathe in the destructive energies, rather than turn away. As humans accept the reality of our adaptive unconscious, they may be more amenable to trusting the flash of their gut instinct that fires the warning flare. Once alerted, their conscious mind would over-ride the allure of mind-control weaponry. Initially, we may need to heed the flash of warning quickly and quietly, allowing our conscious mind to easily recognize dangerous frequencies. Realities are constructed through repeated experience. Certainly the mind-numbing experience of television has made us accustomed to the hazards of mind control and what it takes to rein in and rebalance our health.

Moviegoers discriminate immediately between Aeon and Catherine Zeta Jones. Animated figures, even with the advent of programs like Endorphin, cannot perfectly replicate human dynamics. It feels a bit "off." And so it may be with our next generation of mind weaponry. A part of us will "know" and will react safely.

The advent of exoconsciousness seems connected to dramatic galactic, Earth, and human technologies that affect the human body and consciousness. We are players in a consciousness shift, literally pushing ourselves to the edge of the precipice. If we leap, we may discover we can fly. We are wired for a second chance. Perhaps we can remember a future when we lived in the reality of the second chance.

Others among us, extra- and inter-dimensional, may fly alongside. A homing vibration directs our flight.

All participate in the evolution of human consciousness. We may feel we are alone. We are not. It is time to pull the thread of our extraterrestrial consciousness from our subconscious and weave our ancient knowledge into our present moment. It is time to behave as though we possess an exoconsciousness. We are dimensional beings, held by an inter-dimensional and extraterrestrial lineage that we can access and depend upon. Our human race is not prodigal. Our human race is connected and nurtured in oneness with our origins.

No way is it a secret military aircraft. First, they would not expose something like that to the air traffic control radar and hundreds of witnesses. Second, that thing was in violation of several FAA rules by hovering low over an airport without clearance. Military pilots do that at the risk of their career. It is not done. If the military wants to keep a new aircraft secret, they fly it in zones where public aircraft and the public are restricted.
Aerospace executive response to the documented UFO sighting at O'Hare International Airport, November 2006

CHAPTER 16
BEYOND THE LIGHTS

Did you see the Phoenix Lights? I am frequently asked this question. The answer is no. My exoconsciousness experience is not lights-oriented or focused on craft investigation and documentation. The focus of my research is multi-dimensional reality via consciousness.

Yet, many of my colleagues witnessed the Phoenix Lights and as a result have undergone a profound transformation of their consciousness and belief systems. I respect the UFO lights phenomenon research that anchors ufology. When universities are ready, an academic body of UFO research is available for the lucky generation of students who will chart our pathway to galactic citizenship. Light and craft sighting research complements consciousness research. They are facets of the same phenomenon. They are doorways to a transformation of consciousness and the evolvement of humans into a space-faring, extra-and inter-dimensional species.

The Extraterrestrial Reality class at Scottsdale Community College included a broad historical overview of craft sightings and the political response to extraterrestrial visitation. Students gained respect for the unsung heroes who expanded UFO craft investigation into a respected arena of research. For those attracted to contact experience or intrigued by UFO sightings, an academic framework that includes history of ufology, exopolitics, diplomacy, and exoconsciousness are essential.

So what or who are these lights and craft? First, the UFO phenomenon of craft or light vehicles not manufactured by humans is not new. Sightings have been recorded, though not rigorously analyzed by current scientific standards, for thousand of years. Peter Davenport of the UFO Reporting Center has sighting records from Egypt in 1770 BC and China in the 12th Century AD. Researchers like Peter Davenport and George Filer maintain ongoing archives of present day sightings.

Another frequently asked question. Will there be a mass sighting? Yes, there will be and are ongoing mass sightings such as the Phoenix Lights and the Mexico City flotilla. It is a not a new or a dramatic phenomenon for students of ufology. Craft sightings and light phenomenon are historically commonplace and continuing.

Will UFO's come to our rescue or invade our planet? Will there be a dramatic mass landing to awaken humans? Probably not. Extraterrestrial contact by experiencers repeatedly emphasizes the need for the human race to be vigilant of planet earth. Extraterrestrials have not rescued us from ourselves, yet they keep trying to communicate the need for us to preserve, protect, and nurture our planet and the human species. Yes, dramatic sightings take place across the globe—particularly in Mexico and South America. Jaimie Maussan's popular presentations provide jaw-dropping panoramas of fleets of UFO's moving across Mexican skies. Is this an invasion? Technically, no, because no violence occurs. Yet, this remains a sensitive point with national defense. Countries are territorial about their skies and increasingly defensive about planets they explore and hope to colonize.

I advise releasing the drama and panic of sightings, contact, and mass landings. Sightings and contact, when monitored on a global scale are commonplace and continuing. Human propensity toward drama shuts down access to our subconscious mind that assists in the integration of anomalous experience. Our subconscious mind easily and effortlessly integrates unusual experiences and information. Fear driven trauma shuts off our integration circuitry. We have been and continue to be visited. It will not cease; if anything, sightings are increasing.

Teaching Extraterrestrial Reality pointed to the ebb and flow of sightings. Historically certain periods experienced a rash of sightings, while other periods were calm with minimal activity. Human social/political actions such as war, military research and use of atomic energy provided stimulus for an extraterrestrial response. It was almost as if human development accelerates and they show up. Certainly WWII and the subsequent post-war years were an era of high sightings. According to Michael Wolfe, a controversial figure in ufology who claimed to work with an MJ12 subcommittee and the National Security Council, in 1941 there was a reported crash retrieval by the Navy in the ocean off San Diego. In his book, *Catchers of Heaven,* his data indicated the craft was retrieved with dead Zeta Reticulans (probably grays) inside. The occupants and craft were transported to Wright Patterson Air Force Base and later relocated to Indian Springs. Wolfe hypothesized the crash was due to our discovery and use of pulse radar.

Paola Harris, Italian photojournalist and major figure in exopolitics, interviewed Wolfe prior to his death and maintains his archival information. Her influential book, *Connecting the Dots: Making sense of the UFO phenomenon,* includes an extensive interview with Michael.

Richard Dolan in his seminal work, *UFO's and the National Security State:*

Chronology of a Cover-up 1941 and 1973, traces numerous wartime sightings. These sightings heightened with the famous 1942 UFO "Battle of Los Angeles." Between 15 and 20 unidentified craft flew over Los Angeles and caused a power black out. According to Dolan, the US Army fired 1,430 rounds of anti-aircraft shells, which resulted in 6 human fatalities and destruction of homes and buildings, yet no damage to the flotilla of craft.

WWII also sparked continued interest and exchange of stories among pilots and UFO investigators of *"Foo Fighters."* Foo Fighters were anomalous aerial phenomenon experienced by pilots and crew. Stories included planes monitored or trailed by balls of light. Occasionally these balls of light actually flew through the plane, causing electrical systems to fail. Other times the lights simply trailed the aircraft or toyed with their flight pattern.

Following the devastation of the atomic bomb there was another period of high activity. Three weeks after the atomic bomb, 12 air force specialists approaching Iwo Jima reported 2 tear-shaped, brilliant white objects on a course next to their plane. As reported by the pilots, their navigation systems faltered and engine faltered. Yet, as the lights disappeared, the irregularities ceased.

Post WWII, the lights phenomenon continued. Sightings of Ghost Rockets, or cigar shaped craft, increased across Europe. According to Dolan, our government initially attributed the ghost rockets to German technology such as the V rockets. By 1947, sightings further escalated with pilot Kenneth Arnold's sighting in Boise, Idaho of 9 (number coincidence?) objects moving in a column, with no tails, in formation, going backwards! UFO reports intensified around the time of Arnold's sighting. Numerous citizens came forward with reports: an

Oregon prospector saw 5-6 metallic discs over the Cascade Mountains; numerous sighting reports came in from Kansas City, Oklahoma City, Albuquerque, Canada, Australia, and New Zealand; scientists at the White Sands Proving Ground witnessed a silvery disc. Then in the summer of 1947, the renowned crash(es?) occurred at Roswell. To this day, it remains one of the most meticulously researched crashes, and yet according to mainstream journalists and academicians, the jury is still out. See for yourself. Read Colonel Corso and William Birnes' *The Day After Roswell: A Former Pentagon official reveals the U.S. Government's Shocking UFO Coverup.*

One of the most intriguing sightings was recorded over Washington, DC. According to Richard Dolan and Steven Greer there were sightings two weekends over the nation's capital. The first sighting was July 19, 1952 when radar at Washington National Airport reported a formation of 7 objects near Andrews Air Force Base, moving over 100 mph. A second sighting was the following weekend on the evening of July 26, 1952 when the UFOs returned and were witnessed by a pilot and stewardess of a National Airlines Flight. The public clamor as a result of the sightings triggered a Washington Press Conference where the Air Force held its largest and longest press conference since the end of WWII. During the press conference the Air Force attributed the sighting to the weather related phenomenon of temperature inversion.

As the Office of the President changed hands from Truman to Eisenhower, ufologists traced the importance of the Robertson Panel that was purportedly formed to debunk UFO sightings and keep research in appropriate hands. And yes, as a result, UFO information remains managed to this day. Yet as a result of the sightings and the government's controlled response, a proliferation of civilian research groups soon began to coalesce. In the near future, historians, academic researchers, and university curricula will explore the essential role of citizen researchers such as Coral Lorenzen and her husband, Jim, who founded APRO, the Aerial Phenomena Research Organization; Leonard Stingfield who formed CRIFO, Civilian Saucer Research, Interplanetary Flying Objects; and Townsend Brown who established NICAP, National Investigations Committee on Aerial Phenomenon. All these heroes functioned via phone and mail networks, diligently traveling to investigate sightings and meticulously collecting information. Their work is our archive. Their work is our UFO legacy.

Throughout the world, UFO sightings continue on what seems a daily, continuing basis. Most sightings are not reported, yet with the internet and instant communication, archives are growing. Each spring in Phoenix, thanks to Dr. Lynne Kitei and others, we celebrate the advent of the Phoenix Lights, a triangular shaped craft, reported to be a mile-long, which flew across the state the evening of March 13, 1997. As Dr. Lynne reported in her award-winning film *The Phoenix Lights*, the March 13, 1997 sighting was not a unique event. In the film, Dr. Lynne documented footage of similar light formations years prior to the main sighting in 1997. And sightings of similar V-shaped lights and triangular craft continue to be reported to archivists like Davenport and Filer.

A core of committed sky watchers resides in Phoenix. Many of these sky watchers live multi-dimensional lives where sightings function as the cord between their earth-life and other dimensions. Terri Mansfield, who witnessed the lights with her hospice group in 1997, translates her experience into a peace in space initiative, which she integrates into her work as a co-founder of the Arizona Department of Peace. As the effects of her sighting experience transform her belief system, she strengthens as an internationally acclaimed Peacemaker. Peace on Earth. Peace in Space. Peace Within.

Phoenix citizens continue to monitor the skies and discriminate balloons, satellites and aircraft from unexplained lights or craft. Scott Icenogle, a security guard, monitors the skies near the Deer Valley Airport north of downtown Phoenix. His videotapes provide archival footage for investigators. Jeff Woolwine, who lives with his son, at the base of South Mountain in Phoenix, developed a unique perspective: Woolwine observes light and craft phenomenon from the convenient vantage point of his kitchen window. Those sightings swirling around South Mountain spurred him to walk the mountain trails, scrutinizing drawings of the ancient Hohokam prehistoric tribe who roamed our valley then mysteriously disappeared. Through his website, www. petroglyphsinthesky.com, Woolwine cites the fascinating correlation between ancient rock petroglyphs and current sightings. Using technology, his website displays what he has identified as ancient UFO art, overlaid with his personal sighting videos. According to Woolwine, the light drawings of the ancients of our valley morph into light forms visible today.

Whether individuals watch the skies or walk the carved trail of the ancients or one day awaken to their ability to communicate with beings from another dimension—lives transform as a result of contact with anomalous phenomenon. Lives change, communities form and our belief systems adjust with the input of new information and experiences. Consciousness evolves into Exoconsciousness.

Craft Copula of Consciousness

After many years of varied multi-dimensional contact, I experienced another pivotal shift in my exoconsciousness. A path opened, one that clarified an experience that, until then, was only faintly visible. I term it a "not yet memory". For much of my life I carried a deep memory fragment of being part of a group, a classroom. I had brief glimpses of schooling—a disciplined structure, other students, advisors, and administrators. I carried dim memories of my frequent pulsed transport into a craft. My conscious mind often recreated the pulse and my physical body felt the movement, down and then up into the craft.

One Sunday afternoon, with neither a plan nor a formed desire, I opened the memory while working with a hypnotherapist. Fragments suddenly fell into place. Puzzle pieces fit.

Using a hypnotherapy technique, she guided me into a room of my choice. I immediately entered a lighted room where the walls were alive. Literally breathing and moving. I was a three-year-old child, and so naturally, I played with the walls and they responded with changing colors and forms. A familiar advisor was in the room with me, a male, 10 to 12 foot tall light being. He had huge hands with four fingers. As we visited and reacquainted, I squirmed, remembering my childhood experiences with him. I related to him as a three-year-old human, comfortable in the room, yet active and curious. It was difficult to sit still. He told me that I was there because of an agreement made prior to coming into this life. I had an earth agreement to cooperate with education on this craft. My agreement was to participate in the school to reactivate "star" knowledge that I must have lost at birth.

Then he led me back into a familiar classroom where each student had a seat and an "assignment." It was a small student body, perhaps 24. I felt each one's assignment—they were to grow up to become politicians, musicians, scientists, physicians, inventors, writers, spokespersons. I felt my seat, my assignment. In the classroom, as on my bedroom ceiling, they taught an intergalactic language. The curriculum also included mind and energy work as well as hands-on healing. The craft school was administered by a group of races from Tau Ceti, Andromeda, Pleiades, Acturians, Zeta, Orion, Syrian, Lyra. Students were either from a specific race or hybrids of several races. I saw myself as a tall, slender light being—a lengthy human lightening bug. I felt hybrid, yet primarily Andromedan. Primarily, I was simply a "being." A being beyond race. A being seeded into a human body.

As I moved out of the classroom, I came to a small conference room where three administrators greeted me—a principal and two off-ship visitors. They did not have names. I simply recognized them by their vibration. Each had a signature vibration.

As we reviewed why I was on board and my assignment, I became aware that officials from the military and government would occasionally be invited into our proceedings. They were usually quiet, if not a bit overwhelmed. They unobtrusively stood at the back of the classroom and watched the proceedings. I remembered a woman, one of the off-ship extraterrestrial visitors, reminding all the students to "treat the government representatives with respect." I recalled the craft school gave polite reception to Earth officials, aware of the gap between rambunctious seeded children and adult government officials assigned to understand a new, unfamiliar curriculum. Officials had to learn a new language and participate in a program that we children re-membered with ease. The craft was more fun than work. Instinctively, I recalled a government name for the craft school—the Young People's Project. Or perhaps it was, the Young People's UFO Project. Galactic officials ran the school and graciously permitted others to visit. It was a diplomatic arrangement I knew little about.

At one point in conversation with the three administrative beings, I asked why my life had moved through such dramatic twists and turns. They quickly replied that it was required that I be "authentically human." Afterward, I kept repeating the phrase, "I am authentically human." Earth life was no short-cut, walk-on role. I needed to be fully immersed in human reality.

Then as they escorted me out of the room, I ran up into my favorite place on the craft, the cupola. In the cupola I was privileged to navigate the craft. As I stood at the helm, my mind shifted into a relaxed glide, my small hands one with the craft. I navigated the craft through space. Star maps were stored in my conscious mind. I navigated easily among star systems. Like the Jaime Maussan video, I intuitively knew how to navigate as well as launch and receive craft. The cupola was home. My consciousness fit the craft. We were one.

Back on Earth time and space, I realized that my space contact began around 1954 or 1955. (The same period as Eisenhower's alleged alien treaties.) During the 1950s, ufologists identified contactees who experienced peaceful, kind interactions aboard crafts. Researchers called the aliens who created these visitations "space brothers". I might add that there were equal numbers of "space sisters". Only later, during the 1960s did ufologists begin to characterize the contact experience as abduction and detail harrowing incidents of kidnapping and trauma. Investigators such as Steven Greer (2006) attribute traumatic abductions to deliberate government black operations designed to create fear of aliens in the mass consciousness. He maintains that segments of our secret government possess UFO craft, genetically designed alien look-alike clones and electronic weaponry to stage a believable abduction.

As individuals come to me, eager to bring their multi-dimensional contact into conscious light, I am compassionate and respectful of varied experiences. Each experience is different. Each human bears a distinct seed that opens and flowers into work that only they can perform this earth life. We each have a classroom seat. We each have an assignment. Alliances may form between contactees as they strengthen their work. The contact experience is multi-dimensional, and as such, is as vast as the universe that created each of us. Humans are a holograph of the universe. Your consciousness is at the helm. You know the way.

Birthing your Extraterrestrial

Humans are extraterrestrial. Historically, our extraterrestrial character commenced with the first earth orbit of Russian explorer Colonel Gagarirn, on through countless space missions, lunar, Mars, and space station landings. All of us—astronauts, mission personnel, and citizens participating via radio, television, and internet became extraterrestrial. Though your feet are planted on the Earth, through the space program, you also live multi-dimensionally, as an intelligent being, outside the Earth's atmosphere. You are an extraterrestrial, participating in a space-faring culture.

Your extraterrestrial nature is manifest in your exoconsciousness. It penetrates your mind, body, and spirit.

Humans did not become extraterrestrial over night. It was a process. As a species, we once dwelled in the cocoon of Mother Earth, until 1961 when we broke the bonds, launched by our race into space.

In her book *Butterfly,* Norie Huddle uses the transformation that occurs when a caterpillar becomes a butterfly and relates it to human transformation. During chrysalis, a caterpillar develops new cells called imaginal cells. These cells vibrate at a different frequency. With two frequencies in one body, inevitably, dissonance emerges. Initially, the caterpillar's immune system identifies the new cells as foreign and destroys them. But the Pacman scenario doesn't last long. Eventually as new cells multiply, more and more survive and begin to clump together into groups. With friendly groupings, their frequency strengthens. Eventually these groups form long strings. Then at some point, a tipping point, the cellular message is clear—a new being is present. A butterfly emerges.

A similar phenomenon occurred when humans ventured into space. Amid the excitement, there was dissonance. Skeptics questioned the expense. Adventurers criticized the bureaucracy. Citizens railed at the tragedies. Activists sidetracked funds to their favored programs. Missions were cancelled. Funds diverted.

Still the space program moved forward. In full view and behind closed doors, humans progressed into space, becoming extraterrestrial. Hollywood joined the act. Movies colored culture's imagination as to how extraterrestrials behave and what we could expect as we travel space and live among the stars. The UFO movement launched its own theories of ET technology, visitation, races, motivations, agreements, and alternative historical timelines. Television premiered *Heroes* with super human abilities. Groups of ideas and like-minded people gathered; links connected. One after the other. New life was born. New identity broke out and blossomed. You are no longer defined by the cocoon of Earth. You are Extraterrestrial.

Transformational Exercise

Benefits of this exercise:

- Allowing your body to nurture and encourage new being
- Feeling a new frequency

This morning a friend called. She told me of a frightening nightmare. Someone was breaking into her house. In the dream, she protected herself and locked all the doors. Though the dream was over, she felt distraught. I asked if the fear for her safety was connected to early childhood issues. She thought a moment, and then said yes. We spoke for about old fears and why they seem to resurface. "Will they ever be removed?" she asked. I reminded her of the caterpillar becoming a butterfly.

Try this exercise next time you feel stress, trauma, anger, or sadness. Try this exercise next time you wonder whether old fears will ever be released. Try this exercise when you are ready to transform.

Lie down and consciously recognize all the "new" and "transformational" cells in your body. For example, cells of health, happiness, peace, wealth, love, safety, and security. Identify the opposite of whatever is causing you distress. Or, you might consciously recognize new cells that hold potential for exoconsciousness: intuition, telepathy, healing, bi-location, astral and time travel, manifestation, and creation.

Once your imaginal cells are identified, begin to consciously feel them strengthening. Feel your body pulsing with a new frequency. Then begin to cluster these cells into families or groups. Feel the power and friendship develop among these cells. Next, link these groups into strong chains. One linked to the other. Feel these chains of new imaginal cells define your body. Finally, imagine your personal tipping point, as you become a transformed being. You are an exoconscious, extraterrestrial being.

We all move on the fringes of eternity and are sometimes granted vistas through the fabric of illusion.
Ansel Adams

CHAPTER 17
RE-LEASE AND RE-FORM

Exoconsciousness wanders among worlds. Realities are like a series of photographs in different frames. Time and Space create our primary Earth frame. Yet, there are others.

The ***space-time continuum***. What is it? Where is it? When is it? Do time and space exist or are they illusions we use to weave the fabric of our reality? Do we simultaneously dwell within and without time and space?

As a hypnotherapist, I practice regression techniques, where through hypnosis, a client accesses a "past life" or as I like to refer to it, "another life." Outside our space-time continuum one can access an enlarged perspective of their life. Regression feels as though life is suddenly viewed as a panorama of peripheral vision. We remain anchored to the here and now of our daily life, yet infused with knowledge of other lives. Lives unfold that were once creased and hidden like a childhood paper fan. Regression opens the folds and intricate detail emerges.

I have personally regressed into numerous past lives. Some frightening, some peaceful, some perfectly reasonable. Well…of course I lived in Egypt. I frantically dug in those sands and imagined myself among those stones since childhood. Well…of course I lived among the ***Cathars*** of Southern France, my first taste of French cuisine was memorable. Art, cuisine, literature, music, story, geography all pull us to places we once knew, cultures we once loved or despised.

Numerous times I witnessed regression sessions that provide clients with the perfect answer to a once unsolvable riddle of their lives. Yet, the reality of regression and the information brought forth is outside the space-time continuum. Never, never land. The beyond where our consciousness knows the way.

Travel beyond time and space is our extraterrestrial legacy. You were born to leap beyond the bounds of earth while living on its soil. Do these exoconscious abilities get tricky? Of course. Just like any other ability. The first time you ride a bike or spin a yo-yo—for a time you cannot stop. It's too much fun. Hypnosis and regression can become too much fun. Bring on the past lives, or other lives. As a result you risk becoming lop-sided, living in other dimensions, filtering your present earth experience through the lens of "other lives." Unraveling the mysteries of other times. During a hypnosis session, I once moved quickly into past lives. Having done repeated regressions, it was effortless. The therapist surprised me by commenting that individuals proficient in past lives often live too much in the past to the detriment of the present. Point well taken.

Doing exoconscious work , you need a measure of Buddhism to remind yourself to remain anchored in the present. How fitting that in an era of regression, *astral travel*, levitation and teleportation—the sounds and sayings of Buddhism echo the importance of the present. Here and now.

Alongside hypnotic regression, astral travel and teleportation offer intriguing experiences beyond the time-space continuum. While I have not teleported (physically), I experience repeated astral travel and refine my skills with repeated attempts. As a child I slipped effortlessly into astral travel. Whoosh I was out and about. Then I became an adult and closed the doorway of my conscious mind—babies to raise, responsibilities to assume, a home to tend. Eventually something niggled in my mind—a faint memory of travel beyond my dreams where I was conscious and navigated my path into, through, and out of astral realms. So I began to relearn what came naturally as a child.

In her book, *Out of Body Experiences: A Handbook*, Janet Lee Mitchell (1981) outlines the methods to access out of body experiences (OBE). They include sleep and dreams, which include unconscious OBEs, especially dreams of falling or flying. Lucid dreaming takes dream memory to another level by accessing conscious dreams, where the dreamer remembers details of the experience upon awakening. During lucid dreaming, the dreamer realizes they are in a dream and yet, they do not wake up. They begin to control the dream experience, choosing actions and responses while still dreaming.

The experience of extreme fatigue may also breakdown the body's consciousness and ease the transition into OBE. The astral body may leave the exhausted physical body to recharge it with cosmic energy. Shamanic rituals often invoke extreme exhaustion to ease the OBE. Drugs may be a doorway to conscious expansion, yet don't seem to directly engender astral travel. While drugs are often touted as astral-friendly, a test of 247 LSD users who had OBE experiences showed that under the influence of drugs they were out of body only three to four percent of the time. Others tests have shown that LSD and mescaline may promote an increase in body temperature which produces OBE (Mitchell, 1981, p. 20).

Extreme sensory deprivation through Ganzfeld conditions or meditation and hypnosis decreases the body's motor output and transforms the consciousness to altered states of being. Trauma and psychological stress also trigger altered states of consciousness.

However the method that OBE is achieved, the elasticity of the mind in astral travel corresponds closely with theories of quantum consciousness. In quantum consciousness theory, particles and waves change form when observed, moving forward and backward in time, and occupying two places simultaneously. The physical self remains the anchor as well as the propellant for conscious travel. The legendary silver cord, connecting the conscious to the physical body, points to the necessity of a continuing healthy flow of physical energy to continue the OBE. Upon death, consciousness departs the body and no propellant remains to call back the conscious craft.

At home in the astral plane, consciousness adopts quickly to a quantum reality beyond the limits of time and space where the will moves the craft. OBE experiencers report the ease of chosen destination movement directing their consciousness. Further, unfamiliar or frightening astral dimensions are easily dispelled with a mere thought projection to another destination. Throughout the OBE experience the physical body, or the mother ship, remains the monitor. The traumatized astral traveler can always move back into the safe haven of the physical body.

In 1999, International Academy of Consciousness (IAC) developed a sophisticated online survey and analyzed 98 different aspects of OBE. Well over 7,000 people responded. The international survey showed that OBE had many shared characteristics with people around the world irrespective of age, gender, nationality, ethnicity, cultural background, religion, and education. The IAC continues its research by refining an investigative instrument to understand the processes by which an individual captures information through OBE and remote viewing. They want to investigate both the capturing of the information and the subsequent transfer of information into the physical brain (Gustus, 2004).

Several distinct phenomena are present during an OBE that leads to an expanded awareness of the powers of human consciousness. These phenomena are:

"Self-bilocation—in which the person perceives himself to be in two places at once," (for example, seeing one's physical body).

Self- permeability—in which the projected individual is able to move through physical objects.

Internal autoscopy—in which the individual has an internal view of his or her own body and can see bones and organs, either with the consciousness inside the brain, or outside the physical body.

Cosmoconsciousness—a state of highly expanded awareness, in which the individual perceives the order, balance and logic of the universe, simultaneously feeling and celebrating that he or she is part of it. Nirvana, Satori and Samadhi.

Precognition—in which the individual, fully projected from the physical body, obtains information relating to events that have not yet occurred.

Retrocognition—in which the individual, fully projected from the physical body obtains information relating to events that have already occurred, in this life or a past life.

Extraphysical telepathy—in which the projected individual communicates with others who are in the physical, projected, or nonphysical condition through transmission of thought" (Gustus, 2004).

The OBE occurs in an astral reality between the physical and extraphysical or consciousness bodies. It is not a dream, although it may be triggered by a dream state. OBE reports indicate active participation during the projection—making decisions, using mental attributes, and creating travel itinerary. The environment encountered, though of another dimension, has a distinct reality. The projector is in a reality separate from the physical body and may observe his or her own body and be aware of both the launch from and the landing back into the physical body. As theories of quantum consciousness take root in culture, individuals will readily open to astral travel or OBE experiences. Growing databases of experiences add to the scientific knowledge of our body as mother ship and its consciousness craft. Like knowledge of the automobile engine, individuals will not wait for complete understanding of quantum consciousness, before test-driving their consciousness.

Teleportation

In 2005, cosmologist and astrophysicist Eric Davis completed a paper for the United States Air Force arguing that teleportation was an achievable technology and a legitimate science. "Specifically the purpose of his study was to collect information describing the teleportation of material objects, providing a description of teleportation as it occurs in physics, its theoretical and experimental status, and a projection of potential applications" (Witcher, 2005).

Davis compiled five futuristic viable modes of teleportation. They are:

a) Quantum teleportation is a technique that shifts the characteristics, but not the location of sub-atomic particles at great distances (Witcher, 2005).

b) **Wormholes**, a highly theoretical possibility whereby the intense gravitational field near black holes could rip open entrances to distant locales (Vergano, 2004).

c) Parallel Universe travel in parallel dimensions.

d) Science fiction based Star Trek transporter beams, which he dismisses.

e) Psychic Teleportation, which Davis sees as the most reasonable starting point. Chinese researchers have demonstrated test subjects teleporting fruit flies and grasshoppers with their minds alone (Witcher, 2005). Famed and defamed psychic Uri Geller reportedly teleported a sealed crystal compound out of existence.

Dangers of human teleportation loom large. The "original you will be destroyed, and a new you would emerge elsewhere. It will take a brave person to try that one the first time. No one knows if the essence of you would be preserved" (Knapp, 2005).

The point of Davis' research was to bring together all the existing research on teleportation so that other researchers might use it as a springboard. When the Chinese boast success, the US Air Force and American research institutes at Stanford and Princeton are not far behind with their classified consciousness research.

The power of consciousness to merge with and move matter, once the subject of extraterrestrial themed movies and extraordinary contactee reports, is now within the realm of possibility with military, aerospace applications.

And yet, teleportation triggers questions. Are humans destroyed, and then recreated in teleportation? If so, through the teleportation destruction process, what remains to be recreated?

I believe that as eternal and entangled with the universal consciousness, it is impossible for a teleported human to be destroyed. If we learn through teleportation that we are not destroyed, then beliefs change. Our essence, I would submit, our consciousness, remains. Teleportation research may transform our destruction and death belief system into a belief system of continuous creation. As such, scientific research into teleportation, whether by the military funded, university experiments or individual spiritual experiences presents the opportunity to make a leap. A conscious leap. A leap into experiencing our bodies as conscious, intelligent, eternal, energy systems.

To take the leap and teleport, we need to identify the launching pad within our body. I believe the body's teleportation launching pad is located in the cradle of our Kundalini energy. This Kundalini energy equates to a zero-point, anti-gravity propellant. It launches our consciousness craft to travel and learn while silently waiting our return and redocking. An important exoconscious ability is learning to rock our consciousness out of its cradle in order to travel, teleport, and then redock.

Conclusions

Experts in UFO sightings report extraterrestrial craft as disappearing, instantly reappearing, hovering silently for extended periods of time, dividing into separate spheres, multiplying, and as launching and returning to a mother ship. These extraterrestrial craft behaviors reflect the power inherent in human consciousness—levitation, teleportation, time anomaly, and astral projection. The highest potentials of your human consciousness indicates an exoconsciousness. You are child of the stars.

Developing and using this exoconscious ability to its highest potential requires attention and commitment to move forward in the following areas.

Awakening: First you must commit yourself to the development of exoconsciousness. This requires that you strengthen your desire for an awakening experience to open your exoconscious power. This awakening may be generated by a religious discipline such as yoga, tantra, or body-mind-spirit ritual; a near death experience; or a conscious UFO sighting, contact experience, or communication. All experiences generate the same results, exoconsciousness is awakened.

Living in and acceptance of an Exoconscious Reality: Once you are in an exoconscious reality, you no longer question the presence of other dimensions and other intelligent beings be they on the Earth, galactic, or universal. Your needs shift from proof to acknowledgement and rapid learning occurs through communication and openness.

Release: Once you shift into an exoconscious reality, you experience the dissolving of worn out suppositions, fears, inhibitions, and prejudices. The traditional bounds of earth existence are transcended. Emotional release involves letting go of the storehouse of accumulated energies that no longer serve your highest good. Mental release involves letting go of worn out assumptions and beliefs that no longer work. The clearing of ineffective mental attitudes allows the adoption of a new set of beliefs, such as quantum consciousness, that are concurrent with an exoconscious, multi-dimensional reality. Physical release involves relaxation through the transition. Attention and care of your physical body heighten the energy level, which allows the transformation of DNA to create a physical vehicle for the propulsion of your exoconsciousness.

Building a bridge: During this phase of transition it is essential for you to create a bridge between your earth-self and your expanding exoconsciousness. Time and patience are required for the development of exoconsciousness "space legs." Management and development of your physical body during this process can be assisted by mind-body-spiritual disciplines such as tantra and yoga.

Parallel Dimensions: Once you move into acceptance of an exoconscious reality, you simultaneously accept parallel dimensions where assistance and guidance by star beings may be accessed. We are of the stars and the stars are of us. They are your DNA, your consciousness, and your bloodline. As you ascend into your highest potentials, all beings rise in unison. Acceptance of your safe entrainment to their spiritual energies leads to easy, effortless movement.

Subjective Experience: David Chalmer's Hard Problem of experience holds the solution. Committed to exoconscious development, you learn through trial and error, trust, and relaxation that inner subjective experience is the key to transformation. Guides and advisors line the way as you determine your path. Each path is distinct and different. Inner subjective experience of the Earth's sensory world, the proto-consciousness membrane, and exoconsciousness hold the answers to every question. Intuitive knowing accelerates as subjective experience flows into consciousness.

The power of the physical body propels your consciousness craft into inter-dimensional worlds where your exoconsciousness inheritance can be experienced through travel and communication with the realms that are one with us.

APPENDIX I
HYPNOTHERAPY, COACHING, AND EXOCONSCIOUSNESS

What is hypnotherapy?

Hypnotherapy applies hypnosis techniques that calm the conscious mind to access the subconscious, allowing it to communicate and guide the client. Hypnosis accesses the natural state between wakefulness and sleep, similar to a daydream. When you experience reaching a destination without conscious recall of how you arrived, the phenomenon is called "hypno highway."

Hypnosis uses the power of the mind, in cooperation with body, emotions, and spirit for recovery and health. It works by removing emotional, physical, spiritual, and mental blocks (either conscious or unconscious). Hypnotherapists regard blocks as negative energy forms that penetrate your beliefs, behaviors, and body. These negative or detrimental energies can be transformed or removed. This process is similar to removing a car part that no longer works and replacing it with a new, functioning part. Once blocks are removed, then the hypnotherapist lays positive suggestions created by the client into their subconscious. The subconscious mind welcomes positive suggestions and forward movement. The client transforms easily into new beliefs and behaviors.

Can anyone be hypnotized?

"All hypnosis is self-hypnosis." The level of relaxation and therefore the altered state of consciousness accessed depends on the individual. It is a highly subjective experience. Usually you achieve deeper hypnotic states working with a hypnotherapist over time. It is essential to realize that in a hypnotic state the conscious mind is never completely switched off. You remain conscious and aware.

Why do clients use hypnotherapy?

Hypnotherapy addresses a variety of life issues. Some familiar symptoms you may have include:

I feel like life is passing me by.

Whenever I try to change, something blocks me.

My addiction controls my life.

If I could be pain free, how could I live my life?

My fear feels like a wall that I cannot cross or break down.

Missing memory fragments create sorrow, confusion or holes in my life.

How do I know which path to take?

How does hypnotherapy differ from counseling or therapy?

In hypnotherapy, it is the client's subconscious and suggestions, not the therapist, that guides and directs the method of inner healing. With the assistance of the hypnotherapist, you can tap into your unique source of guidance, health, and happiness in order to move in a desired direction. Hypnotherapists do not categorize symptoms or classes of psychological behaviors. Each individual is regarded as connected to a subconscious source of holistic health.

How does Coaching work with Hypnotherapy?

Coaching and Hypnotherapy are complementary. As hypnotherapy removes blocks, your life moves forward. Coaching offers a practical framework that strengthens desired changes. Coaching affords a relationship where you envision a new life and form achievable goals and objectives. Coaches pose powerful questions that open you to a new perception of yourself and your reality. With permission, the coach holds you accountable for agreed upon actions and commitments that add up to significant life changes.

How does hypnotherapy work in conjunction with medical treatment?

Hypnotherapy is a complementary therapy that promotes rapid acceleration of medical treatments by releasing and transforming beliefs or behaviors. Hypnosis works effectively with the part(s) of you that are fearful of change, helping you to relax and move into a new way of life.

For example, under a physician's counsel to change your lifestyle (exercise, diet, smoking, or drinking), you might use hypnotherapy to ease and accelerate the transition. If you experienced compulsions and addictions and were under the care of a recovery program, physician, or therapist, you might use hypnotherapy to ease behavioral changes.

Hypnotherapy is also effective for management of pain and anxiety as well as calming the patients prior to surgery. It can also be used to:

Enhance Performance and Creativity

Recover from Addictions

Manage Weight, Pain, and Sleep

Achieve Relaxation and Remove Stress and Anxiety

Enhance Happiness and Self-Esteem

Remove and resolve painful Memories

How is Hypnotherapy used to reclaim memories?

An interesting aspect of hypnotherapy is the subconscious ability to move beyond the time-space continuum to access memories and information. Since the subconscious mind is operating beyond ordinary time and space, it may be that reclaimed memory fragments are sourced in a parallel reality, occurring in a simultaneous reality. Or, memory fragments may be energies attached during life experiences, the mass consciousness, or culture.

Regardless of the source, you may experience memory fragments as coming from your childhood past or what is termed a past life. Past lives may simply be energies of the mass consciousness you hold in your mind, body, and spirit that under hypnosis you choose to remove, release, and resolve. Sometimes these memories are painful and you may experience relief and peace as a result of the session. The energy of fear, punishment, and anxiety attached to the memory is removed and peace is restored.

Hypnotherapy for reclaiming memory is effective for abuse and trauma survivors as well as persons who feel a "void" or a keen awareness that "something is missing." Reclaiming memory assists you in putting together the puzzle pieces of your life. Often people experience the feeling that "now, everything makes perfect sense."

How is Hypnotherapy used to access our Exoconsciousness?

Hypnotherapy, combined with reading, research, as well as spiritual and physical work, often results in an ability to consciously access exoconsciousness and begin to use its power.

Hypnotherapy is especially effective in reclaiming memory of interaction with extraterrestrial or intelligent beings, activity off-planet or in other dimensions such as the underworld. As my mentor, Ruth

Hover, claims, a person's anomalous experience usually says more about the person than the experience. In other words, you filter your extraterrestrial encounter experiences through your subjective attitudes, beliefs, and behaviors. As John Mack acknowledged, you move through a spiritual experience as you comprehend and integrate a contact experience. You remove the fear and enter a new reality.

Hypnotherapy is useful to access multiple dimensions of reality. As you explore realities, you gain confidence and clarity. You experience yourself as a multi-dimensional being. Realities once restricted by religion, culture, or superstition are accessible and you learn that each is simply one of numerous dimensions available. Multiple sources of energy and information come on-line as you experience the vast dimensions of consciousness. Likewise, you develop a deep appreciation of the potential, power, and scope of consciousness while living in a human body on the Earth. And, in turn, you experience the supportive, harmonious, relational aspects of Universal consciousness. Actions and beliefs take on new meaning in relation to other humans, the planet Earth, and the Universe.

APPENDIX II
STAR KID/STAR SEED IDENTIFICATION
QUESTIONNAIRE

© 2003 by Richard Boylan, Ph.D.

vers071703

(Note: This Questionnaire may also be used by adults suspecting they are Star Seeds.)

Directions: Circle score number at end of each question answered "yes", and add up the scores at the end.

Rating Schedule:

Score of 12= probably a Star Kid

Score of 16 = most likely a Star Kid

Score of 20+ = absolutely a Star Kid

1. The child has a larger than average head for his/her age and height, especially in the front or top of the head. = 1

2. The child has an average body temperature of below 97.6 F [36.4 C] degrees = 1

3. The child's birth was notable for there being a strange presence or figure in the delivery room. or an aura (glow) noted around the child or their crib. = 2

4. The child began saying a number of words clearly by six months of age (at least one year before the average talking age of 18 months.) = 1

5. The child began walking by one-half-year-old (before the average walking age of one year old.) = 1

6. When the child began speaking, s/he used phrases or whole sentences almost immediately, not just single words = 1

7. People notice that the child seems extremely mature for their age, almost like an adult in a child's body. = 1

8. In childhood the child sought out more advanced activities, being bored with and underchallenged by the games the other children his/her age wanted to play. = 1

9. The child mentioned recalling his/her "other parents" out among the stars, or expressed a longing to go back to his/her "real home" out in the cosmos. = 2

10. The child's gaze seems unusually mature and penetrating/knowing. = 1

11. The child's entire childhood is notable for growing up very much faster physically and intellectually than the other children the same age. = 1

12. The child is very sensitive, and is put off by, or shrinks away from the destructive, mean, cruel, violent, or wasteful behavior of the other kids, and cannot understand why they are that way. = 1

13. Sometimes, when the child goes by an amber sodium-vapor-plasma streetlight, the light goes out, particularly if the child is emotionally charged = 2

14. The child exhibits mental telepathy (silent mind-to-mind communication). = 1

15. The child has more than once foretold something in the future that later actually happens, or has a "Dream" which later comes true (precognition). = 1

16. The child has made an object move by focused mental concentration effort, such as influencing a pinball game, a basketball shot, or a bowling ball's direction. =1

17. The child can mentally see something going on at a different location, or in the past, or in the future (clairvoyance/remote viewing). = 1

18. The child acquires new information spontaneously, apparently by mental "downloading", either in awake-state awareness or by being shown things during sleep. = 1

[If the child knows the data came from Star Visitors, =2]

19. The child is adept at cross-species communication, both knowing what an animal (e.g.., pet dog, a dolphin, etc.) is thinking, and communicating telepathically with that animal, and the animal responds to the silent communication. = 1

20. The child "just knows" something intuitively about a person, a place, or a situation, which then turns out correct, (i.e., the child is "psychic"). = 1

21. The child affects certain electrical appliances repeatedly by his/her mere presence, (such as a TV changing channels, a radio turning on, a wristwatch not working any more, or a lamp turning on or off without touching it) = 1

22. The child has admitted using mental thought to influence the behavior of another, and is effective at this silent influencing (e.g. a parent for a second dessert helping) = 1

23. The child reports seeing Visitors that the parents/others cannot see, or sees things out of the corner of the eye which disappear when stared directly at; (inter-dimensional viewing). = 1

24. The child can see auras around other people or animals (quasi-visible energy fields, often visible with Kirlian photography). = 1

25. The child sees or feels color, patterns or "textures" in those auras, which provide information about the other's health, emotional state, psychic attunement, etc. = 1

26. The child is able to use psychic diagnosis (intuitive "seeing", or passing a hand above the patient's body) to correctly locate an area of illness, injury, or disease. = 1

27. The child uses internalized energy (psychic energy/prana/chi/cosmic force) and directs it outward to the place on another person's/animal's body that needs healing, and that person/animal very soon experiences improved health.=1

28. The child has made him/herself "invisible", either by relocating elsewhere by mental effort, or more commonly, by causing those around not to notice that the child is present. When the child "turns it off", others suddenly notice him/her. = 1

29. The child has caused an object to relocate from one location to another without touching it [teleportation], or made it rise from the ground and move [telekenesis], solely by mental effort and intention. = 2

30. The child has been observed at least once to self-levitate (rise several inches or more above the ground), whether intentionally or spontaneously, = 2

31. The child engages in actions, rituals, or ceremonies of their own design which are intended to impart healing to a person, an animal, a plant, or a particular place on the Earth. = 1. [If the child has brought a completely-dead animal, plant, person, or ecological area back to life by such healing, then the score for this question = 5.]

32. The child has deliberately influenced time by causing an event, such as a road trip, to complete very rapidly (e.g., a 1-hour trip in ½ hour, without speeding up). = 1

33. The child has caused a lengthy event to occur in a brief time, by the clock; (e.g., in 15 minutes events stretch out so that everyone believes an hour had passed. = 1

34. The child can tell when a future event, (e.g., an earthquake, car accident, a fire), is going to happen, warns others about the event, which then occurs. = 1

35. Sometimes at night the child's consciousness/personality goes elsewhere, via out-of-body/astral travel), (even though the physical body remains in bed,) and returns later and reports experiences had elsewhere. = 1 [If visits the Star Visitors, = 2]

36. During waking state the child has traveled out-of-body to have experiences elsewhere. Those near the child merely note that s/he seemed "tuned out". The child later returns with recollection of these experiences elsewhere. = 1

37. The child has served at times as a communication channel for off-planet intelligences, and has some awareness of which Star Visitor is speaking through him/her. = 2

38. The child reports visits by the Star Visitors (ET's).= 1

39. The child's parent(s) have had visits by the Star Visitors. = 1

40. The child reports that the Star Visitors are family from an earlier existence. = 2

41. The child has experienced at least one episode of sharing their mental space with a Star Visitor, who utilizes the child's mind and body for limited periods to experience life on Earth. = 1

42. The child has demonstrated the capacity to summon one or more Star Visitors or their spacecraft (UFO) successfully, and they later show up as requested. = 1

43. The child is obsessed and driven with a sense of special mission on Earth, even if that mission is not yet entirely clear to the child at the present time. = 1

44. The child exercises unusual adult-like initiatives for the social good, (such as contacting their Senator or a television personality to present a plan for achieving peace in a specific situation); or, if an adult, uncharacteristically begins such world-healing activities. =1

45. The child reacts with an unusually intense positive recognition or emotion to realistic photos or drawings of Star Visitors in magazines, on television, or in a movie. = 1

46. The child after age 6 hardly ever gets serious flus or other illnesses that sweep through their classroom or neighborhood [increased infectious resistance], and heals extremely rapidly from cuts, fractures, and other injuries, or, some Star Kids go the alternate path: are extremely sensitive to environmental contaminants, the sensitivity expressed as allergies, and have low digestive tolerance for certain substances (for instance, cannot tolerate dairy products, are mildly allergic to even whole-wheat products, and find meat-eating repulsive) , or develop disorders (labeled as "Asperger's", ot "Attention-Deficit Hyperactivity") which suggest an incompatibility between their neurological wiring and the nervous system of regular Humans. = 1.

47. The child has an unusual eye iris color, or iris pattern, or pupil shape, or overall eye configuration in the head. = 1

48. The child is drawn at an early age to a non-church natural spirituality which incorporates reverence for the Earth as a living organism/consciousness, the sacredness of life in all creatures great and small, and an awareness of the cosmic reach of life. = 1

49. The child, without any coaching, has a natural affinity for correctly using crystals, energetic stones, or other power objects to amplify psi energy, e.g., for healing purposes. = 1

50. The child has complained about wanting to "go home" elsewhere and feeling alienated from the coarseness of Earth society and typical human behaviors. = 1

51. The child is strongly drawn to other Star Kids, and they, too are also strongly drawn to and feel an affinity with the child as a Star Kid. = 1

52. Score only ONE of the following two Sub-Questions [(a) or (b)]:

(a). The child does exceptionally well in school, easily mastering subjects without much or any study, is bored with the pace of instruction in most schools, and is comfortable in a learning environment well ahead of his age, (e.g., an elementary student taking high school classes, a high schooler doing college or graduate work, or a child bored in a Gifted School;) = 1[or]

(b). The child is misunderstood by the school system, mislabeled "Attention Deficit Disorder" or "Learning Disability" (because s/he is bored, under-challenged, or put off by the "normal" children's learning pace); or mislabeled "Hyperactivity Disorder" (because of fidgetiness in the classroom out of boredom, or because of their thoughts directed to more challenging subjects, or because the child is highly focused on a topic of interest and perseveres much longer than is considered "normal"); or mislabeled "Learning Disabled" (because s/he sees and points out the connections between the subject being taught and other subjects, (such as history-math-science-art connections) when the teacher only wants to hear about the one subject being taught.) = 1

53. The child has experienced a "Walk-In" or replacement of the original human (dying) personality by a new (off-world) personality, which takes on the existing body and continues the life, having memory of earlier years but with different abilities and personality = 1

54. The child has an unusually large bioelectromagnetic-photic field extending outward from their body, (e.g., over 3 feet [1 meter]), as measured by dowsing rods.= 1

<><><><><><><><><><><><><><><><><><><><><><><><><><><><><>

If the child (or adult) scores 12 or above, please suggest to the parent that they contact Dr. Richard Boylan, Director, Star Kids Project©, about further information available on Star Kids or Star Seeds, and about a Workshop for them, families and friends, so that they can better understand the phenomena, grow more comfortable with their advanced abilities, and to meet other Star Kids and families, and clarify their Star Kid/Star Seed mission.

Richard Boylan, Ph.D., LLC, P.O. Box 1009, Diamond Springs, CA 95619, USA.

1-(530) 621-2674. drboylan@sbcglobal.net

Websites: www.drboylan.com and

http://www.drboylan.com/starkididqstnr.html

Richard Boylan, Ph.D., LLC

Behavioral scientist, exo-anthropologist, researcher, hypnotherapist

Director, Star Kids Project©

Post Office Box 1009, Diamond Springs, California 95619, United States of America.

Phone: (530) 621-2674 (PDT)

E-mail address: drboylan@sbcglobal.net

Website: www.drboylan.com

GLOSSARY

ABDUCTION: Kidnapping of humans by extraterrestrials for the purpose of communication or medical examination. Distinguished from **Contact** or **Experience** that reflect a more benevolent, less traumatic interaction with extraterrestrials. By their own volition,

Contactees and **Experiencers** may cooperate with extraterrestrials.

ALANON: 12-step recovery program for families and friends of alcoholics.

ALLOPATHIC MEDICINE: Modern medical approach using multiple drugs to treat
patients for symptom relief.

ANNUNAKI: Sumerian Gods and Goddesses, also referred to as **Elohim** and **Nephilim**.
In Genesis referred to as "those who from heaven to earth came."

ARTIFICIAL INTELLIGENCE, AI: AI considers knowledge a commodity stored in a machine. When this machine based knowledge is applied in a practical way it constitutes intelligence. Computer technology is used to build intelligent machines. Based on the 1960's view of the brain as a computer.

ASTRAL TRAVEL: An experience, either spontaneous or induced, of separating your astral or spiritual body from your physical body, which permits conscious travel through space, time and other dimensions. The astral body remains corded to the physical body.

AURA: A multidimensional energy surrounding and penetrating the physical body. Energy levels within the aura include the physical, etheric, astral, mental, causal, and spiritual.

BOOK OF ENOCH: A pseudoepigraphal work, omitted from the Old and New Testaments. Authored by a biblical character on behalf of fallen angels.

CATHARS: 12th and 13th Century Gnostic religion, predominately in Southern France, described as "pure ones." In 1208 the Pope launched the Albignesian Crusade followed by the Inquisition to destroy the Cathars.

CHAKRA SYSTEM: Subtle, spinning energy system in the body that may affect its chemical, cellular, and hormonal composition.

COACHING: Relationship between client and coach focusing on business, professional or personal growth, by posing powerful questions, setting goals, and emphasizing strengths in order to move forward.

CONSCIOUSNESS: State of being conscious and alert. The opposite of unconscious. Susan Blackmore defines consciousness as knowing or attending to something, subjectivity.

CROP CIRCLES: Areas of flattened and swirled of crops mixed with standing plants to form intricate, geometric patterns. Source or cause of circles remains under investigation.

CYBERNETICS: Term meaning "art of steering," used in 1947 by Norbert Weiner to describe a system using models of organization, feedback, and goals to understand the composition and dynamics of any system. Information is a result of interaction.

CYTOSKELETAL MICROTUBULES: Microtubules are protein structures that are components of the cytoskeleton, the internal framework of a cell.

DEAD SEA SCROLLS: Scrolls and scroll fragments found between 1947 and 1960 in caves near the Dead Sea. Contained Hebrew

Scriptures and information on Hebrew culture prior to the birth of Jesus.

DNA TRANSPOSONS: "Jumping DNA" sequences of DNA that move around in the genome of the cell, causing mutations.

DOWNLOADS: Information downloaded directly into an individual's mind, experienced as a subtle energy transfer.

ELECTROMAGNETISM: Physics of electricity and magnetism. Magnetism developed by a current of electricity.

ENTANGLEMENT: Physics principle that quantum states of two objects are related despite their separation in space.

EXOCONSCIOUSNESS: Author's 21st century concept describing study of the extraterrestrial origins, experience, abilities, and multiple dimensions of human consciousness.

EXOPOLITICS: Michael Salla defined Exopolitics as the study of the key political actors, institutions, and processes associated with the UFO phenomenon and extraterrestrial hypothesis.

Alfred Webre defined Exopolitics as the science of relations between our Earth and advanced intelligent civilizations in the Universe.

FOO FIGHTER: Name used by Allied pilots during WWII to describe anomalous aerial phenomenon, such as darting glowing orbs, that followed and at times entered aircraft.

GNOSTICISM: Early religious movement claiming secret, hidden knowledge. From the Greek work *gnosis* meaning experiential knowledge, or intuitive insight. A collection of Gnostic texts are in the **Nag Hammadi.**

GRAYS: An extraterrestrial race predominately gray in color. Small Type A grays from Zeta Reticuli and Orion are hairless beings with large wrap-around dark eyes, large heads, thin torsos, and three fingers.

HEARTMATH: Organization founded in 1991 by Doc Childre, offering technology to transform and reduce stress. Based on the link between heart, emotions, and mind in human performance.

HOLOGRAPHIC PRINCIPLE: Every part of a hologram contains information of the whole. Three dimensional hologram is created by the interference pattern of two laser beams interacting.

HOMEOPATHIC MEDICINE: Based on the law of similars, using microdosesof natural substances, matching treatment to symptoms.

HUMANOID: Extraterrestrial race nearly indistinguishable from humans. Described as having near perfect features with blue eyes and blonde hair, six feet tall. Origins of human looking races include Pleiades, Sirius, and Orion. Also referred to as Nordics.

HYPNOSIS: Derived from the Greek word for "sleep". A method of accessing altered states of consciousness using relaxation, expectation, and suggestion. Effective for releasing emotional blocks, changing behavior patterns, recovering memory, and accessing the subconscious mind for guidance and clarity.

JOHREI: A subtle energy, similar to **Reiki,** used for self-realization and healing. It was developed by Mokichi Okada (who had been a student of Mikao Usui, the developer of what later came to be called **Reiki**) in the 1930s.

JUNK DNA: Segments of DNA along a chromosome that do not code for genes, non-coding genes. Comprise upwards of 95% of human genome.

KABBALAH: Body of mystical Jewish teachings interpreting hidden meaning in Hebrew scripture.

KIRLIAN PHOTOGRAPHY: Russian electrical engineer, Semyon Kirlian, developed a photographic process to capture bioenergetic processes of living systems on film.

KUNDALINI: Sanskrit word for "coiled." An energy that lies dormant at the base of the spine until awakened and channeled by breathing or yoga.

MAJESTIC 12 OR MJ12: Alleged covert committee formed in 1947, after **Roswell,** during the Truman Administration. A committee of scientists, military, and government responsible for investigating UFO activity and eventually managing disclosure.

MEMBRANE THEORY: The premise that all matter in the universe is connected to a unified, vast structure, or a membrane.

NAG HAMMADI: A collection of ancient Gnostic texts, including the Gospel of Thomas, discovered in Egypt near the town of Nag Hammadi.

NEURAL LINGUISTIC PROGRAMMING: NLP: Discipline developed by John Grider in the 1970s, focusing on how communication impacts and is impacted by subjective experience. Reliance on development of practical therapy tools.

NIBIRU: Planet X or the Planet of the Crossing, referred by Sumerian texts to have an expansive 3,600 year orbit within our solar system. As it travels closer to earth and the planets within our solar system, it carries a field of debris which may trigger meteorite damage.

NUMEROLOGY: Study of the meaning of numbers, dates, and number values of letters. In Greek and Hebrew alphabet, each letter represented a number. Numbers had significance in human affairs.

OPERATION PAPERCLIP: Following the collapse of Nazi Government, a WWII intelligence operation formed to collect and disperse German scientists into the United States who specialized in rocketry, chemical weapons, mind control, and medicine.

ORBS: Balls of energy that may change color or light, travel at high speeds, squeal, or hover. Appear to possess an intelligent energy. Frequently visible in digital photographs.

PHOENIX LIGHTS: The mass sighting of a large, possibly mile-wide, V-shaped UFO craft that traversed the skies of Arizona on March 13, 1997. Dr. Lynne Kitei is a key witness and researcher of this event. She produced the award-winning film, *The Phoenix Lights*.

PRAYING MANTIS: Extraterrestrial beings with thin long torsos, distinguished by arms and legs that bend at mid-joint, displaying a graceful crouched pose. A gentle intelligent race.

PROTO-CONSCIOUSNESS: According to philosopher, David Chalmers, consciousness is a fundamental property of all matter, a natural part of the physical laws of the universe.

QUANTUM PHYSICS: A branch of physics studying the energy characteristics of matter at the sub-atomic level.

REIKI: A subtle energy, naturally present in the human body, used for self-realization and healing. A method for directing this energy was developed in the early 1900s by Mikao Usui, who called it a method for achieving personal perfection.

REMOTE VIEWING: The ability to consciously access information at a distance from geographic locations, persons, and events, by following a protocol including coordinates of the desired target.

Developed by team of researchers who included Ingo Swann and Russel Tarq at Stanford Research Institute.

REPTILIAN COMPLEX: A primitive part of the brain linked to survival and self-preservation, source of aggressive and territorial behaviors.

REPTILIANS: A tall extraterrestrial race identified by scaly skin, yellow slit eyes, and blunt, large noses. Reportedly a highly advanced race with a hierarchical society.

ROSWELL: In July of 1947, on a farm outside Roswell, New Mexico, was the reported crash of alien space craft. Allegedly, debris was brought to Roswell's Sheriff and the Roswell Air Force base was notified. The *Roswell Daily* Newspaper carried three stories, the first one announcing possession of a flying saucer. Investigation continues.

SCHUMANN RESONANCE: A set of spectrum peaks in the extreme low frequency portion of the earth's electromagnetic field. Lowest frequency is approximately 7.83.

SLEEP PARALYSIS: A momentary, frightening paralysis experienced while waking up or falling asleep. Symptoms may include levitation, awareness of intruders, noises, and smells.

SPACE-TIME CONTINUUM: A physics model that combines and simplifies space and time into a single construct. Time is usually seen as the third dimension and space as the fourth dimension.

SINGULARITY: Term used in 1993 by computer scientist, Vernor Vinge, and popularized by Ray Kurzweil to describe a future dominated by superintelligence aided by **artificial intelligence**, computer-brain interfaces, and technologically assisted **consciousness**.

TANTRA: An ancient esoteric Hindu/Buddhist spiritual practice of breath and energy work. Sanskrit for "loom" or weaving.

TALL GRAYS: Extraterrestrial race reportedly from Orion. Five to seven foot tall with large noses, mushroom brown skin, dark blue eyes, and fine hair on their head.

TALL WHITES: According to Charles Hall (2002), "They had the usual thin frail body build, chalk white skin, large blue eyes, and nearly transparent platinum blonde hair. Like all of the tall whites, their eyes were perhaps twice the size of human eyes and they stretched noticeably further around the sides of their heads than human eyes do."

TELEPORTATION: A method of transportation where matter or information dematerializes and then recreates at a different location.

TEMPLAR: A knight in the religious order of Knights Templar or Knights of the Temple, established in 1118 to protect pilgrims traveling to the Holy Land. Alternative historians speculate the Templars recovered artifacts from King Solomon's Temple.

UFOLOGY: The study of unidentified flying objects, UFOs.

UNDERWORLD: Metaphysical, inner-dimension of the Earth. Inhabited by mythical creatures such as fairies, reptiles, elves, and alligators. Egyptians believed humans entering doorways to the underworld followed paths that led to the stars. All dimensions are inter-connected, inter-related.

WALK-IN: Ancient Hindu concept, adopted by New Age thought, describing a body where the original soul is removed and replaced by a new soul. Individuals report being the subject of an extraterrestrial walk-in.

WORMHOLES: Hypothetical portals or tunnels in space, linking vast distances.

BIBLIOGRAPHY

Arntz, William and Betsy Chasse and Mark Vicente. (2005). *What the Bleep do we* Know: Discovering the Endless Possibilities for Altering your Everyday Reality. Health Communications.

Barlow, Dilly. (2002, February 2). Parallel Universes. *BBC Interview.* http://www.bbc.co.uk/cge-bin/education/betsie/parser.pl/0105.

Beckett, Don. (2005). *The Entrance, The Deep Inside, The Mystery: An Exploration of Usui Reiki and Beyond.* Reiju Tree. Electronic book available *at http://new-reiki-books.johreiki.net/.*

Begich, Nick. (2006). *Controlling the Human Mind: The Technologies of Political Control or Tools for Peak Performance.* Earthpulse.

Blackmore, Susan. (2004). *Consciousness: An Introduction.* Oxford: University Press.

Brennan, Barbara. (1993). *Light Emerging: The Journey of Personal Healing.* New York: Bantam.

Bruce, Robert. (1999). *Astral Dynamics: A New Approach to Out of Body Experiences.* Virginia: Hampton Roads Publishing Company.

Boylan, Richard. (2004, January 5). Star Seed Characteristics. Message posted to UFOFacts@yahoo.com. (2005). *Star Kids: The Emerging Cosmic Generation.* http://www.drboylan.com/booksad2.html.

Chopra, Deepak. (1990). *Quantum Healing: Exploring the Frontiers of Mind/Body Medicine.* New York: Bantam.

Clancy, Susan. (2007). *Abducted: How People come to Believe they were Kidnapped by Aliens.* Harvard University.

Clark, Rosemary. (2000). *The Sacred Tradition in Ancient Egypt*. Minnesota: Llewellyn.

Collins, Andrew. (1996). *From the Ashes of Angels: The Forbidden Legacy of a Fallen Race*. Vermont: Bear & Co.

Collins, Anne. (1998). *In the Sleep Room*. Lester & Orpen Dennys Ltd. Collins, Robert and Richard Doty. (2006). *Exempt from Disclosure: Site 51,S4, MJ-12, Wright-Pat, Los Alamos*. Peregrine Communications.

Corso, Phillip, and William Birnes. (1997). *The Day After Roswell*. New York: Pocket.

Dolan, Richard. (2002). *UFO's and the National Security State: Chronology of a Coverup 1941-1973*. Virginia: Hampton Roads.

Edelman, Gerald. (2004). *Wider than the Sky: the Phenomenal Gift of Consciousness*. Yale University Press.

Emoto, Masaru. (2005). *The Hidden Messages in Water*. New York: Simon and Schuster.

Enoch. Book 1. Watchers. 1 25, 2005, http://earth-history.com/Pseudepigrapha/Enoch/enoch-1-watchers.htm.

Fleming, Nick. (April 11, 2005). Experts put a health warning on 'electrical allergy' advice. http://www.telegraph.co.uk/core/content.

Fretheim, Terence E. (1994). Genesis: An Introduction, Commentary and Reflection. *The New Interpreter's Bible*. Nashville, TN: Abingdon Press.

Gardner, Laurence. (2003). *Lost Secrets of the Sacred Ark: Amazing revelations of The Incredible Power of Gold*. London: Element.

Gerber, Richard. (2001). *Vibrational Medicine: The #1 Handbook of Subtle Energy Therapies*. Vermont: Bear.

Gladwell, Malcolm. (2005). *Blink: The Power of Thinking without Thinking*. New York: Little Brown.

Greer, Steven. (2001). *Disclosure: Military and Government witnesses Reveal the Greatest Secrets in Modern History*. Virginia: Crossing Point. __. (2006). *Hidden Truth Forbidden Knowledge*. Virginia: Crossing Point. ustus, Sandie. (2004). Out-of-body experience: a powerful tool for self-research [Electronic version]. *Nexus Magazine, 11*.

Hall, Charles. (2002). *Millennial Hospitality*. 1ˢᵗ Book Library.

Harris, Paola Leopizzi. (2003). *Connecting the Dots: Making Sense of the UFO Phenomenon*. North Carolina: Wild Flower Press. (2006) *Exopolitics: How does one speak to a Ball of Light? Exopolitical Challenges And Protocols for Future Contact*. Indiana: Authorhouse.

Hart, Will. (2003). *The Genesis Race: Our Extraterrestrial DNA and the True Origins of the Species*. Vermont: Bear & Company.

Henry, William. (2005). *The Illuminator: Mary Magdalene, Solomon's Key and the Lost Secret of the Templars*. Nashville: Scala Dei.

Howe, Linda Moulton. (2001). *Glimpses of Other Realities: High Strangeness, Vol II*. ___. www.earthfiles.com.

Huddle, Norie. (1990). Huddle Books.

Huff, Dan. (2005, May). Quantum consciousness? Welcome to the mind-boggling world of mind-brain research. Leave your tired, old assumptions at the door. *Tucson Weekly*. http://www.tucsonweekly.com.

Huyghe, Patrick. (1996). *The Field Guild to Extraterrestrials: A complete overview of alien lifeforms—based on actual accounts and sightings*. New York: Avon.

Icke, David. (2001). *Children of the Matrix*. Bridge of Love.

Issac. (2007). http://isaaccaret.fortunecity.com/.

Illing, Robert-Benjamin. (2004, January). Humbled by History. *Scientific American,* http://www.sciammind.com/article. cfm?articleID=0003BD0B-ACAC-116D- A7E783414B7F0000.

Kelder, Peter. (1998). *Ancient Secret of the Fountain of Youth, Vol. I and II.* New York: Bantam.

Kelleher, Colm. (1999). Retrotransposons as engines of human bodily transformation. *Journal of Scientific Exploration,13,* 9-24.

Kettler, John. (2005). The biology of transcendence [Electronic version]. *Atlantis Rising, 52.*

Kilham, Christopher. (1994). *The Five Tibetans: Five Dynamic Exercises for Health Energy and Personal Power.* Healing Arts.

Kitei, Lynne. (2004). *The Phoenix Lights.* Virginia: Hampton Roads.

Knapp, George. (2005, February 9). US explores teleportation. *8 Eyewitness News.* http://klas-tv.com/global/story.

Kuhn, Robert. Is consciousness definable? *Closer to Truth.* http://www. pbs.org/kcet/closertotruth.

Lewels, Joe. (1996, June). The reptilians: humanity's historical link to the serpent race. *Fate Magazine.* http://www.llewellyn.com.

Mack, John. (2000*). Passport to the Cosmos: Human Transformations and Alien Encounters.* New York: Three Rivers Press.

Marrs, Jim. (1997). *Alien Agenda: Investigating the Extraterrestrial Presence Among Us.* New York: Harper Collins.

Maussan, Jaime. *Jaime Maussan and 15 years of UFO Sightings in Mexico.* DVD. http://www.paradigmclock.com/X-Conference/X-Conference.htm.

May, Gerald, gen. ed. (1977). *The New Oxford Annotated Bible with the Apocrypha.* New York: Oxford University Press.

Matthews, Caitlin. (1989). *Elements of the Celtic Tradition*. Dorset: Element.

Mitchell, Janet Lee. (1981). *Out-of Body Experiences: A Handbook*. New York: Ballantine Books.

Myss, Carolyn. (1997). *Anatomy of the Spirit: The Seven Stages of Power and Healing*. Three Rivers.

Naydler, Jeremy. (1996). *Temple of the Cosmos: The Ancient Egyptian Experience of the Sacred*. Vermont: Inner Traditions.

O'Reilly, Scott. (2005). Wider than the sky. *Intervention Magazine*. http://www.interventionmag.com.

Palca, Joe. (November 2005). As Y chromosome shrinks, end of men pondered. http://www.npr.org.

Paddison, Sara. (1993). *The Hidden Power of the Heart: Achieving Balance and Fulfillment in a Stressful World*. Boulder, Colorado: Planetary Publications.

Pennick, Nigel. (1979). *The Ancient Science of Geomancy: Living in Harmony with the Earth*. London: Thames and Hudson.

Picknett, Lynn, and Clive Prince. (2000). *The Stargate Conspiracy: Revealing the Truth Behind Extraterrestrial contact, military intelligence and the mysteries of Ancient Egypt*. London: Warner.

Popnin, Valdimir. The DNA phantom effect: direct measurement of a new field in the vacuum substructure. http://www.xs4all.nl/'ator1341/dnaz.html.

Ring, Kenneth. (1989). Near-death and UFO encounters as shamanic initiations: some conceptual implications. *ReVision, 11*. http://www.nidsci.org/pdf/neardeath.pdf.

Salla, Michael. (2004, January 28). Eisenhower's 1954 meeting with extraterrestrials: the fiftieth Anniversary of America's first treaty with extraterrestrials. *Exopolitics Journal*. www.exopolitics. org.(2004). *Exopolitics: Political Implications of the Extraterrestrial Presence*. Tempe: Dandelion.

Sauder, Richard. (1998). *Kundalini Tales*. Illinois: Adventures Unlimited

Silva, Freddy. (2002). *Secrets in the Fields: The Science and Mysticism of Crop Circles*. Virginia: Hampton Roads.

Sitchin, Zecharia. (1976). *The Twelfth Planet: Book 1 of the Earth Chronicles*. New York: Avon Books.

Starbird, Margaret. (2003). *Magdalene's Lost Legacy: Symbolic Numbers and the Sacred Union in Christianity*. Vermont: Bear. (1998). *The Goddess in the Gospels: Reclaiming the Sacred Feminine*. Bear. (1993). *The Woman with the Alabaster Jar*. Bear.

Stewart, R.J. (1992). *Earth Light: The Ancient Path to Transformation Recovering the Wisdom of Celtic and Faery Lore*. Massachusetts: Element.

Vergano, Dan. (2004, November 5). Air Force report calls for $7.5 M to study psychic teleportation. *USA Today*. http://www.usatoday. com.

Walton, Travis.(1997). *Fire in the Sky: The Walton Experience*. Marlowe.

Webre, Alfred. (2005). *Exopolitics: Politics, Government and Law in the Universe*. Vancouver: Universebooks.

White, Anne Terry. (1959). *All About Archeology*. New York: Random House.

Winslow, Lance. (April 2005). Can we stop cancer from frequency pollution? http://www.ezinearticles.com.

Witcher, T.R. (2005, March 31). Is teleportation possible? And you thought tax dollars were being wasted. *Las Vegas Weekly.* http:// www.lasvegasweekly.com./2005/03/31/awsi.html.

Wolf, Michael. *Catchers of Heaven.*

Zohar, Dana & Marshall, Ian. (2001). *SQ: Connecting with our Spiritual Intelligence.* London: Bloomsbury.

Printed in the United States
136012LV00004B/1/P